# 1 JOHN
# 2 JOHN
# 3 JOHN

ABINGDON NEW TESTAMENT COMMENTARIES

# 1 JOHN
# 2 JOHN
# 3 JOHN

## DAVID RENSBERGER

*Abingdon Press*
*Nashville*

ABINGDON NEW TESTAMENT COMMENTARIES:
1 JOHN, 2 JOHN, 3 JOHN

*Copyright © 1997 by Abingdon Press*

*This book is printed on recycled, acid-free, elemental-chlorine–free paper.*

**Library of Congress Cataloging-in-Publication Data**

Rensberger, David K.
   1 John, 2 John, 3 John / David Rensberger.
      p.    cm. — (Abingdon New Testament commentaries)
   Includes bibliographical references and index.
   ISBN 0-687-05722-1 (pbk. : alk. paper)
   1. Bible. N.T. Epistles of John—Commentaries.  I. Title.
  II. Series.
  BS2805.3.R44  1997
  227'.9407—dc21                                  97–14992
                                                   CIP

97 98 99 00 01 02 03 04 05 06—10 9 8 7 6 5 4 3 2 1

MANUFACTURED IN THE UNITED STATES OF AMERICA

*For*
*My Mother*
*and in Memory of*
*My Father*

# CONTENTS

Foreword . . . . . . . . . . . . . . . . . . . . . . . . . . . . . . . . . . . . . . . . 9

Preface . . . . . . . . . . . . . . . . . . . . . . . . . . . . . . . . . . . . . . . . . 11

List of Abbreviations. . . . . . . . . . . . . . . . . . . . . . . . . . . . . . . 13

Introduction . . . . . . . . . . . . . . . . . . . . . . . . . . . . . . . . . . . . . 17

   Authorship. . . . . . . . . . . . . . . . . . . . . . . . . . . . . . . . . . . . 17

   Historical Settings and Purposes. . . . . . . . . . . . . . . . . . . 20

      Relation to the Gospel of John. . . . . . . . . . . . . . . . . 20

      Setting and Purpose of 1 John . . . . . . . . . . . . . . . . . 21

      Setting and Purpose of 2 John . . . . . . . . . . . . . . . . . 26

      Setting and Purpose of 3 John . . . . . . . . . . . . . . . . . 26

      Dates and Location . . . . . . . . . . . . . . . . . . . . . . . . . . 29

   Literary Characteristics. . . . . . . . . . . . . . . . . . . . . . . . . 30

      1 John . . . . . . . . . . . . . . . . . . . . . . . . . . . . . . . . . . . 30

      2 John . . . . . . . . . . . . . . . . . . . . . . . . . . . . . . . . . . . 33

      3 John . . . . . . . . . . . . . . . . . . . . . . . . . . . . . . . . . . . 34

   Theological Issues. . . . . . . . . . . . . . . . . . . . . . . . . . . . . . 34

      Christology . . . . . . . . . . . . . . . . . . . . . . . . . . . . . . . . 36

      Love One Another . . . . . . . . . . . . . . . . . . . . . . . . . . 37

God in the Epistles. . . . . . . . . . . . . . . . . . . . . . . . . 39

Other Theological Topics. . . . . . . . . . . . . . . . . . . . 40

    Dualism. . . . . . . . . . . . . . . . . . . . . . . . . . . . . . . 40

    Salvation and Sin. . . . . . . . . . . . . . . . . . . . . . . 41

    Eschatology. . . . . . . . . . . . . . . . . . . . . . . . . . . . 42

    The Church. . . . . . . . . . . . . . . . . . . . . . . . . . . . 42

    Tradition and Spirit. . . . . . . . . . . . . . . . . . . . . 43

**Commentary: 1 John**. . . . . . . . . . . . . . . . . . . . . . . . . 45

Prologue (1:1-4). . . . . . . . . . . . . . . . . . . . . . . . . . . . 45
Walking in the Light and Sinning (1:5–2:2). . . . . . . . . . . 49
Walking in the Light and Keeping the Commandments
(2:3-11). . . . . . . . . . . . . . . . . . . . . . . . . . . . . . . . . 58
Conquering the World (2:12-17). . . . . . . . . . . . . . . . . 69
The Coming of the Antichrist (2:18-27). . . . . . . . . . . . 76
Living as Children of God (2:28–3:10). . . . . . . . . . . . . 84
Love and Hatred (3:11-17). . . . . . . . . . . . . . . . . . . . 96
Confidence Toward God (3:18-24). . . . . . . . . . . . . . . 102
Testing the Spirits (4:1-6). . . . . . . . . . . . . . . . . . . . 109
God Is Love (4:7-18). . . . . . . . . . . . . . . . . . . . . . . 116
Loving God (4:19–5:5). . . . . . . . . . . . . . . . . . . . . . 124
Testimony to Jesus the Son of God (5:6-12). . . . . . . . . 130
Final Reflections (5:13-21). . . . . . . . . . . . . . . . . . . . 137

**Commentary: 2 John**. . . . . . . . . . . . . . . . . . . . . . . . . 147

**Commentary: 3 John**. . . . . . . . . . . . . . . . . . . . . . . . . 157

**Select Bibliography**. . . . . . . . . . . . . . . . . . . . . . . . . 165

**Index**. . . . . . . . . . . . . . . . . . . . . . . . . . . . . . . . . . . 173

# FOREWORD

The *Abingdon New Testament Commentaries* series provides compact, critical commentaries on the writings of the New Testament. These commentaries are written with special attention to the needs and interests of theological students, but they will also be useful for students in upper-level college or university settings, as well as for pastors and other church leaders. In addition to providing basic information about the New Testament texts and insights into their meanings, these commentaries are intended to exemplify the tasks and procedures of careful, critical biblical exegesis.

The authors who have contributed to this series come from a wide range of ecclesiastical affiliations and confessional stances. All are seasoned, respected scholars and experienced classroom teachers. They take full account of the most important current scholarship and secondary literature, but do not attempt to summarize that literature or to engage in technical academic debate. Their fundamental concern is to analyze the literary, socio-historical, theological, and ethical dimensions of the biblical texts themselves. Although all of the commentaries in this series have been written on the basis of the Greek texts, the authors do not presuppose any knowledge of the biblical languages on the part of the reader. When some awareness of a grammatical, syntactical, or philological issue is necessary for an adequate understanding of a particular text, they explain the matter clearly and concisely.

The introduction of each volume ordinarily includes subdivisions dealing with the *key issues* addressed and/or raised by the New Testament writing under consideration; its *literary genre, structure, and character;* its *occasion and situational context,* including its wider social, historical, and religious contexts; and its *theological and ethical significance* within these several contexts.

In each volume, the *commentary* is organized according to literary units rather than verse by verse. Generally, each of these units is the subject of three types of analysis. First, the *literary analysis* attends to the unit's genre, most important stylistic features, and overall structure. Second, the *exegetical analysis* considers the aim and leading ideas of the unit, deals with any especially important textual variants, and discusses the meanings of important words, phrases, and images. It also takes note of the particular historical and social situations of the writer and original readers, and of the wider cultural and religious contexts of the book as a whole. Finally, the *theological and ethical analysis* discusses the theological and ethical matters with which the unit deals or to which it points, focusing on the theological and ethical significance of the text within its original setting.

Each volume also includes a *select bibliography,* thereby providing guidance to other major commentaries and important scholarly works, and a brief *subject index.* The New Revised Standard Version of the Bible is the principal translation of reference for the series, but the authors draw on all of the major modern English versions, and when necessary provide their own original translations of difficult terms or phrases.

The fundamental aim of this series will have been attained if readers are assisted, not only to understand more about the origins, character, and meaning of the New Testament writings, but also to enter into their own informed and critical engagement with the texts themselves.

Victor Paul Furnish
*General Editor*

# PREFACE

Living in close contact with the Johannine epistles for several years has affected me in more than one way. I hope it has allowed me to understand why they were written and what their author was trying to say, well enough, at any rate, to bring some clarity to others who study them. For texts so brief, they contain a surprising number of puzzles—linguistic, literary, historical, and theological. I found myself wondering more than once why "the elder" chose to express himself so obscurely, when clarity would have been just as ready to hand. I have not sought to conceal from the reader those places where it seems impossible to be certain exactly what the text means. I have tried to make a decision in every case, but I hope I have not left the impression that I am offering the definitive solutions to these problems. I hope also, however, that I have been able to offer more than a series of problems and solutions. The opportunity to reflect on the theological and ethical implications of these epistles is an opportunity to consider the meaning and interrelationship of Christian faith and love. Here too I have tried not to hide what seem to me problematic directions sometimes taken by the epistles; but I have also sought to point out the ways in which these texts, on the periphery of the New Testament canon, sometimes touch on the heart of its message. Without encroaching on the territory of the theologian and the preacher, I have aimed at least to enable them to confront these issues as I have found myself confronting them.

I am grateful to the editors of this series for allowing me to go somewhat beyond the commentary's original allotted length, in light of the peculiar difficulties, different for each epistle, that it had to address. Even so, I am only too well aware of the many points on which it has not been possible to say enough, and the even greater number of places where I could not sufficiently indicate my debt to previous scholars. In keeping with the format of the series, the bibliography indicates only works that I have actually cited, and only those commentaries offering more detail than this one for those in search of further information (but also a few smaller commentaries that seemed particularly worthy of inclusion). Of the many scholars for whose work I have a high regard, I can mention only two here. No one can study the epistles or the Gospel of John without expressing admiration for the achievement of Raymond E. Brown. If I have ventured to differ with him on this or that point, it is only within the framework of a thoroughgoing appreciation for the direction and the standard that he has set for the future of Johannine studies. A scholar whose approach has been rather different from that of Brown, and yet who has done invaluable service for students especially of the two small epistles, is Judith Lieu. Again I cannot agree with every one of her conclusions, but I have found her original and carefully thought out studies highly stimulating.

I must record my gratitude to the staff of the Atlanta University Center Robert W. Woodruff Library, who so skillfully and diligently handled my many requests. I am also indebted to Victor Paul Furnish, general editor of the *Abingdon New Testament Commentaries,* for his detailed and judicious reading of the manuscript. A semester's sabbatical leave from the Interdenominational Theological Center greatly facilitated the completion of my research, and I thank the administration and my colleagues there for that opportunity. During the last stages of this project, my wife Sharon has had to do without the support that her own overworked professional life ought to have had. I am thankful to her, as always, for putting up with the countless distractions of my work.

David Rensberger

# LIST OF ABBREVIATIONS

| | |
|---|---|
| *1 [2] Clem.* | *First [Second] Clement* |
| 1QS | *Manual of Discipline* (Qumran Cave 1) |
| *2 Apoc. Bar.* | Syriac *Apocalypse of Baruch* |
| *3 Apoc. Bar.* | Greek *Apocalypse of Baruch* |
| 1 Enoch | Ethiopic *Book of Enoch* |
| AB | Anchor Bible |
| AnBib | Analecta biblica |
| *Adv. Haer.* | Irenaeus, *Against Heresies* |
| *Ant.* | Josephus, *The Antiquities of the Jews* |
| *Apoc. Pet.* | *Apocalypse of Peter* |
| *As. Mos.* | *Assumption of Moses* |
| AT | Author's translation |
| AUSS | Andrews University Seminary Studies |
| *Bapt.* | Tertullian, *On Baptism* |
| BETL | Bibliotheca ephemeridum theologicarum lovaniensium |
| *BJRL* | *Bulletin of the John Rylands University Library of Manchester* |
| BWANT | Beiträge zur Wissenschaft vom Alten und Neuen Testament |
| *BZ* | *Biblische Zeitschrift* |
| BZNW | Beihefte zur ZNW |
| *CBQ* | *Catholic Biblical Quarterly* |
| CD | Cairo text of the *Damascus Document* |
| CEV | *The Bible for Today's Family* (Contemporary English Version) |
| CNT | Commentaire du Nouveau Testament |
| *Corp. Herm.* | *Hermetic Corpus* |

| | |
|---|---|
| *Decal.* | Philo, *On the Decalogue* |
| *Det.* | Philo, *The Worse Attacks the Better* |
| *Did.* | *Didache* |
| *Diss.* | Epictetus, *Dissertations* |
| EKKNT | Evangelisch-katholischer Kommentar zum Neuen Testament |
| *Exc. Theod.* | Clement of Alexandria, *Excerpts from Theodotus* |
| *Gos. Phil.* | *Gospel of Philip* |
| *Gos. Truth* | *Gospel of Truth* |
| *Herm. Man.* | *Shepherd of Hermas, Mandate(s)* |
| *Herm. Sim.* | *Shepherd of Hermas, Similitude(s)* |
| *Hist. Ecc.* | Eusebius, *History of the Church* |
| HNT | Handbuch zum Neuen Testament |
| HNTC | Harper's NT Commentaries |
| HUT | Hermeneutische Untersuchungen zur Theologie |
| ICC | International Critical Commentary |
| *Ign. Eph.* | Ignatius, *Letter to the Ephesians* |
| *Ign. Smyrn.* | Ignatius, *Letter to the Smyrnaeans* |
| *Ign. Trall.* | Ignatius, *Letter to the Trallians* |
| *Int* | *Interpretation* |
| *JBL* | *Journal of Biblical Literature* |
| *JSNT* | *Journal for the Study of the New Testament* |
| *J.W.* | Josephus, *The Jewish War* |
| KJV | King James Version |
| LXX | Septuagint |
| MNTC | Moffatt NT Commentary |
| NAB | *The New American Bible* |
| NCB | New Century Bible |
| NEB | *The New English Bible* |
| *Neot* | *Neotestamentica* |
| NICNT | New International Commentary on the New Testament |
| NIV | *The Holy Bible, New International Version* |
| NJB | *The New Jerusalem Bible* |
| *NovT* | *Novum Testamentum* |

| | |
|---|---|
| NRSV | New Revised Standard Version |
| NRT | *La nouvelle revue théologique* |
| NTS | *New Testament Studies* |
| Poly. *Phil.* | Polycarp, *Letter to the Philippians* |
| Post. Cain | Philo, *On the Posterity and Exile of Cain* |
| Praem. | Philo, *On Rewards and Punishments* |
| QD | Quaestiones disputatae |
| REB | *The Revised English Bible* |
| *Ref. Haer.* | Hippolytus, *Refutation of All Heresies* |
| *RelSRev* | *Religious Studies Review* |
| *RevThom* | *Revue thomiste* |
| RSV | Revised Standard Version |
| *Sacr.* | Philo, *On the Sacrifices of Abel and Cain* |
| SBLDS | SBL Dissertation Series |
| SBT | Studies in Biblical Theology |
| *SJT* | *Scottish Journal of Theology* |
| *Somn.* | Philo, *On Dreams* |
| *Spec. Leg.* | Philo, *On the Special Laws* |
| *T. 12 Patr.* | *Testaments of the Twelve Patriarchs* |
| *T. Benj.* | *Testament of Benjamin* |
| *T. Gad* | *Testament of Gad* |
| *T. Iss.* | *Testament of Issachar* |
| *T. Jos.* | *Testament of Joseph* |
| *T. Jud.* | *Testament of Judah* |
| *T. Levi* | *Testament of Levi* |
| *T. Reub.* | *Testament of Reuben* |
| TEV | *The Bible in Today's English Version* (Good News Bible) |
| *Tg. Neof.* | *Targum Neofiti I* |
| *Tg. Ps.-J.* | *Targum Pseudo-Jonathan* |
| *Treat. Seth* | *Second Treatise of the Great Seth* |
| TU | Texte und Untersuchungen |
| *TynBul* | *Tyndale Bulletin* |
| TZ | *Theologische Zeitschrift* |
| *Vita Mos.* | Philo, *The Life of Moses* |
| WBC | Word Biblical Commentary |
| *WTJ* | *Westminster Theological Journal* |

| | |
|---|---|
| WUNT | Wissenschaftliche Untersuchungen zum Neuen Testament |
| *ZKG* | *Zeitschrift für Kirchengeschichte* |
| *ZNW* | *Zeitschrift für die neutestamentliche Wissenschaft* |
| *ZTK* | *Zeitschrift für Theologie und Kirche* |

# INTRODUCTION

Among the epistles of the New Testament, 1, 2, and 3 John form a distinctive group. The two small epistles both name their author as "the elder" and are closely similar in form. All three share distinctive features of style and vocabulary among themselves and with the Gospel of John, so that together the four are referred to as the "Johannine writings." (The book of Revelation, different in many ways, is now generally treated separately.) Yet there are also significant contrasts among them. The form of 1 John is entirely unlike those of the Gospel or the small epistles. Its language and theology diverge from the Gospel in numerous ways. Both 1 and 2 John seem to address the same situation, but this situation is fundamentally different from that of the Gospel, while the situation behind 3 John is not clearly related to that of any of the others. We must, then, address the question of how these four documents are related to one another in authorship, historical circumstances, literary form and style, and theology.

## AUTHORSHIP

At least since the second century, Christian tradition has held that these writings were all composed by John the son of Zebedee, one of the twelve apostles. However, neither his nor any other name actually appears as author in any of them, and the historical and theological development evident in them makes it unlikely that they date from the apostolic period. The great similarity in language and thought, especially between the Gospel and 1 John, does makes it seem logical that they were all written by the same person. Yet serious arguments have been presented against this as well, and today many commentators find it unlikely.

There are a number of subtle but serious linguistic differences between John and 1 John (Dodd 1937, 131-41), although there are equally impressive similarities (Poythress 1984). Several factors could account for the differences: 1 John is much shorter than the Gospel, it consists of parenesis rather than narrative and discourse, and it is addressed to a different situation and therefore has different kinds of things to say. Nevertheless, as the commentary will show, even if the author of 1 John writes the same style as the fourth evangelist, he simply does not write it as well. The Gospel of John is characterized by irony and multiple meaning; 1 John tends toward obscurity, using pronouns with no clear reference and ambiguous conjunctions that confuse the linkage between clauses. There are theological differences as well. First John lays more emphasis on Jesus' atoning death and future coming. Important concepts, such as the mediation of Jesus between God and the believer, are treated in noticeably different ways in the two writings. It seems unlikely, therefore, that the same person wrote both the Fourth Gospel and 1 John.

Yet the close relationship between the two suggests that they must at least come from the same circle within early Christianity. Because the Johannine writings do share many qualities that set them apart from the rest of the New Testament, they probably derive from a community with a distinctive history and a distinctive tradition. Some scholars speak of a "Johannine school," that is, a group of teachers and theologians who created and maintained this tradition and produced its literature (Culpepper 1975; Brown 1982, 94-97). Certainly the "we" of the prologue to 1 John is not that of the apostles and eyewitnesses, but of a group that preserved and continued their testimony (see the comments there). Whether or not there was a Johannine "school," it is at least possible that more than one person within the community wrote in the style typical of the Johannine tradition. The style may have originated with the author of the Fourth Gospel and then become the common property of teachers, preachers, and writers within the Johannine community.

The clearest indication of authorship in the epistles is the title "the elder" *(ho presbyteros)* in the openings of 2 and 3 John. Unfortunately, this itself is not very informative. The designation seems to imply a position of respect, but elders as officials in the early church always belonged to a local *group* of elders; there is no parallel for "*the* elder" without a name or location (Lieu 1986, 52-55; despite Donfried 1977, 328-29). Papias, the bishop of Hierapolis in Asia Minor early in the second century, apparently wrote of "elders" as mediators of tradition about Jesus, though his meaning is far from clear (Eusebius *Hist. Ecc.* 3.39.3-4). Other early Christian writers use the term in similar, and even less precise, ways. Papias names a John as one of these elders, and it has become commonplace to reconstruct an "Elder John in Ephesus," distinct from the apostle John, as the tradition-bearer who wrote the Johannine epistles. Judith Lieu, however, has shown just how little foundation for this there is in the ancient texts, and how little connection between what is said of these elders and what we read in 2 and 3 John (1986, 12-14, 55-63). "The elder" thus remains a shadowy figure; even the authority that he seems to claim was clearly capable of being challenged (3 John).

Is this same elder the author of 1 John? Its anonymity might suggest that he is not. The authority of 1 John is that of communal witness, not individual status (Lieu 1991, 23-27). Yet the author addresses the readers as his "children," which implies some personal authority. The similarity in language and situation to 2 John strongly favors common authorship; indeed, the very obscurity of 2 John 6 recalls several passages in 1 John. In the end, though the commentary will point out important differences in language and thought among the epistles, 2 and 3 John are simply too short to provide satisfactory evidence of separate authorship. No theory is capable of definitive proof, and there remain valid reasons for deciding the issue in different ways. Yet the best working hypothesis seems to be that the same author, who was not the author of the Fourth Gospel but was in a position of respect or authority within the Johannine community, wrote all three epistles. Given the masculine title "the elder," this is one of the few cases in which we can be reasonably certain of the gender of an anonymous author, and the masculine pronouns used in this commentary are not generic but reflect this fact.

## HISTORICAL SETTINGS AND PURPOSES

Though the Johannine epistles are included among the "catholic" epistles of the New Testament, that is, those meant for the church at large, it is evident to most readers that they are addressed to specific situations. These situations, and how the epistles address them, prove to be more important than their authorship for understanding and interpreting them.

### Relation to the Gospel of John

The situation of 1 and 2 John is clearly not that of the Fourth Gospel. There the most immediate crisis concerns the expulsion of confessing Christians from the synagogue (John 9:22; 12:42; 16:2). The epistles make no mention of this, and give no indication of any problems directly related to Judaism. The stress on maintaining what has been known "from the beginning" (1 John 1:1; 2:7, 24; 3:11; 2 John 5-6) suggests that the epistles are later writings, looking back to an earlier stage of their tradition. Indeed, some passages in 1 John seem to be based on the Gospel of John, for instance the prologue and the ending (1 John 1:1-4; 5:13; John 1:1-18; 20:31), and the description of the love commandment (1 John 2:7-8; John 13:34). Some of these allusions could be to oral Johannine tradition rather than to the Gospel as the written form of that tradition; but it seems likely that the Gospel was in existence more or less as we know it (perhaps with the exception of chapter 21) when the epistles were written. It has been suggested that some passages in the Gospel, especially in chapters 15–17, are editorial additions made at the time the epistles were written (e.g., Becker 1969, 1970; von Wahlde 1990, 74-104). These passages are consistent with the rest of John, however (Rensberger 1992, 298-302); and 1 John's pattern of ascribing to God attributes that the Gospel ascribes to Jesus (see below) applies to all literary levels of the Gospel, including these.

It is sometimes argued that certain ideas in 1 John, about eschatology and atonement for instance, represent a more "primitive" form of Christian belief than the thought of the Gospel, and therefore that 1 John is actually earlier (Grayston 1984, 7-14). However, both the ideas and the specific terminology in question also appear in works as diverse in date as 1 Thessalonians and 2 Peter, Romans and Hebrews. In fact, this is simply part of another major pattern in 1 John, the use of terms and concepts not found in the Fourth Gospel but common elsewhere in early Christian literature. First John may not only be later than the Fourth Gospel, but may represent an effort to open the Johannine community up to other forms of developing Christianity, just as its opponents were apparently open to other religious currents of the time (see further Dodd 1937, 142-48).

## Setting and Purpose of 1 John

We must note, first of all, that the only evidence we have about the historical situation of 1 John comes from 1 John itself, and since the author did not need to describe that situation in detail for his readers, what we learn of it is mostly by way of allusion. To most scholars, it seems clear that the occasion for the writing of 1 John was a crisis within the Johannine community caused by the people mentioned in 1 John 2:18-27; 4:1-6 (see also 2 John 7-11), and therefore that the text as a whole is to be understood as a response to these opponents. Judith Lieu, however, urges that 1 John is primarily directed within the community, to bring reassurance to its members and to lay out an understanding of difficult aspects of Johannine theology (1981; Lieu 1991, 15-16, 50-51). Yet while the author is certainly not writing *to* the opponents, he does seem to be writing *about* them, and wrestling with difficulties inherent in Johannine theology in the form in which the opponents have brought them into focus. Nevertheless, Lieu rightly reminds us not to lay more emphasis on 1 John's allusions than they can sustain, or neglect the author's positive message to his community.

In the passages noted above (see also 3:23; 4:15; 5:1, 5-13), the author speaks of people whom he calls antichrists, deceivers, and false prophets, who "went out from us" and who fail to confess that Jesus is the Christ and the Son of God, or to confess "Jesus Christ having come in flesh" (AT). Thus, the author is concerned about a group that has left the community and holds a Christology that he finds inadequate. Other statements may be directed against these opponents as well. First John makes strong, if not always consistent, assertions about sin, insisting that those who claim relationship with God must live their lives accordingly (1:5–2:11; 2:28–3:10; 5:16-18). In particular, the author lays powerful stress on love for one another (2:9-11; 3:10-18), which he sees as intimately connected with Christology (3:23; 4:7–5:5). He also asserts more explicitly than the Fourth Gospel that the blood of Jesus brings cleansing and atonement for sin (1:7; 2:2; 4:10). First John 4:1-6 suggests, furthermore, that appeals to the Spirit as the source of christological teaching had become problematic (note also 2:20-27; 5:6-8), and that the opponents were actively engaged in mission.

All these features probably pertain to a single group. In particular, the author not only makes parallel statements about Christology and mutual love (4:7; 5:1, 4-5), but draws a genuine theological connection between them, rooted in the concept of the incarnation as the revelation of the God who is love (4:8-11). This suggests that inadequate Christology and inadequate love both characterize the same group of opponents. However, though love is as prominent as Christology in 1 John, the statements about the latter are far more obscure. Therefore, the nature of the opponents' christological inadequacy must be considered in more detail.

Most who study 1 John conclude that the opponents' failure to confess the "flesh" of Jesus Christ meant a devaluation of his physical, human reality—if not a denial of it altogether, then at least a belief that only his divinity and not his humanity was relevant to salvation (Brown 1982, 75-79). Such a Christology is often called "Docetic," from a Greek verb that means "to seem," applied to a type of second-century Christology according to which Christ seemed to be human but was not really so (Brox 1984). The hints in 1 and 2 John are not enough to identify the opponents as full-fledged Docetists, and it may be best to avoid that label. Still, they may represent an early move toward Docetism. Some of the first known Docetists, whom Ignatius of Antioch criticizes for their denial of the flesh of Jesus, were probably not far removed in time or location from the opponents of 1 and 2 John (Ign. *Trall.* 9-10; Ign. *Smyrn.* 1-7).

It remains unclear how the passages that insist on confession of Jesus as Christ and Son of God fit this view (2:22-23; 4:15; 5:1, 5). Such a confession of faith was precisely what the Gospel of John sought to encourage in the face of the synagogue expulsions (20:31). First John's opponents are Christian, not Jewish, however, and it is not likely that they regarded Jesus Christ as less than divine (as proposed, in various ways, by Grayston 1984, 18-19; Smalley 1984, xxiii-xxv; von Wahlde 1990, 126-27, 138-61). More likely, 1 John's point is to affirm not that Jesus is the Christ, as in the Fourth Gospel, but that the Christ is *Jesus.* The opponents may have focused on the divine Christ as a being distinct from the human Jesus, one who brought salvation from heaven. First John 5:6-8 seems to imply that they saw the baptism of Jesus and the descent of the Spirit as the "coming" of the Christ onto him, and that they played down the significance of his crucifixion (hence 1 John's emphasis on his atoning death). Admittedly, this is not the most obvious way of reading the confessional passages. Yet it is the way most congruent with the general type of Christology that 4:1-3 seems to presuppose. Both the author and his opponents were reinterpreting Johannine tradition in a new situation, and these passages may be appealing to the central confessional statements of that tradition in order to accuse the opponents of contradicting these statements rather than reporting what the opponents themselves actually said.

Cerinthus, who founded a kind of Gnosticism in the second century, did teach that the divine Christ descended on Jesus at his baptism and departed before his crucifixion (*Adv. Haer.* 1.26.1). The opponents of 1 John may therefore at least be related to Cerinthianism (Robinson 1962, 134-36; Wengst 1976, 24-34; Blank 1984, 175-76), especially since second-century legend claimed that the apostle John himself had opposed Cerinthus (*Adv. Haer.* 3.3.4; 3.11.1). However, we do not know that Cerinthus or his followers refused to confess Jesus Christ as "having come in the flesh," and many features of his thought, as it has come down to us, are missing in 1 and 2 John (Brown 1982, 65-67, 766-71; Schnackenburg 1992, 21). There were others in the second century and later who separated the divine Redeemer from the human Jesus (*Adv. Haer.* 1.7.2; 1.15.3; 1.30.11-14; *Exc. Theod.* 61; *Treat. Seth* 51:20–52:9; 56:4-19; *Apoc. Pet.* 80:23–83:15). The Christology of the opponents has points of contact with both Cerinthus and the Docetists in Ignatius, and it is plausible to consider them as at least forerunners of these and other groups, some of them Gnostic (Brown 1979, 151-54; Brown 1982, 104-106; Strecker 1996, 74-76). It may equally well be, though, that they represent a form of belief that has left no other trace in history. One must certainly beware of identifying the opponents as "Gnostics" and then interpreting 1 John in terms of Gnostic traits that it does not even mention (Bogart 1977; Wengst 1976, 37-59).

At present the most persuasive explanation of the dispute behind 1 John is that it was about the interpretation of Johannine tradition (Brown 1979, 93-144; Brown 1982, 69-103; Wengst 1976; Painter 1986). To be sure, not every detail of what 1 John ascribes to the opponents can be easily derived from the Gospel of John. If the opponents claimed that their ideas were inspired by the Spirit, however, they would not hesitate to offer *new* concepts built up from their basic interpretation of the tradition. This is why 1 John calls for the testing of spirits and emphasizes continuity with "the beginning," and why 2 John 9 warns against those who "go forward" (AT).

The controversy probably arose out of changed circumstances in the Johannine community. The Gospel of John, in conflict with the synagogue authorities over the messiahship of Jesus, laid great emphasis on his heavenly origin, contrasted dualistically with "the world" that opposed him. With the passage of time and an increase in Gentile membership, such ideas took on new connotations. The conception of the Spirit as leading the community into new truth (John 14:25-26; 16:12-15) offered broad possibilities. Some members now developed the already high Johannine Christology to an extreme level. Influenced by a more radical dualism, which regarded matter and physicality as inferior to spirit and a hindrance to it, they saw only the divine Christ—the heavenly Son of God—as the bearer of revelation and salvation, whereas the life and death of the Jesus of human flesh was without salvific meaning or value. By the same token, if Jesus' human life was of no consequence, then there need be no connection between salvation and their own daily lives. They may have believed that faith in the heavenly Christ and possession of the Spirit gave them not only spiritual knowledge, an intimate relationship with God, and eternal life, but a divine nature incapable of sin, no matter what their actions. Denying that Jesus' life and death had saving significance, they felt no need for him either as an atoning sacrifice or as a model for loving sacrifice on their own part. Whatever the traditional Johannine commandment to "love one another" meant to them, they did not see spiritual value in concrete acts of care, such as using their material means to help their needy sisters and brothers (3:16-18). Perhaps relatively elite socially, they may have convinced a large number of Johannine Christians to accept their new interpretation of the common tradition and follow them into a separate fellowship, and gained new members from outside as well (4:5).

Some such hypothesis seems necessary to explain the data in 1 John. Yet ultimately our focus must be on the text itself and not on a hypothetical reconstruction, and this leads to the question of the purpose of 1 John. The author says that he is writing to establish and maintain a joyful fellowship, to prevent the readers from sinning, and to assure them of eternal life (1:3-4; 2:1; 5:13). These general statements gain meaning from the specific warnings and exhortations that surround them, however. It is the opponents who threaten the fellowship and assurance of the community, and risk leading it into sin. The author's positive intentions could only be achieved by warding off the attractions of these "deceivers" (1:8; 2:26; 3:7). The purpose of 1 John, then, is to strengthen the readers in their fellowship with the author and with the tradition of christological witness and active love that he represents, by assuring them that in remaining in this fellowship they do indeed remain in relationship with God and with Jesus Christ, and so have eternal life.

# Setting and Purpose of 2 John

Second John gives the impression of being a kind of summary treatment of the same issues as those that 1 John handles, with the emphasis on Christology. Unlike 1 John, however, 2 John proposes a concrete course of action to be taken against the opponents (vv. 10-11). Not all scholars accept this impression at face value. Theories of 2 John as a literary fiction will be considered below. Georg Strecker has proposed that 2 and 3 John are the *earliest* Johannine writings. According to Strecker, 2 John 7, which speaks of "Christ *coming* in the flesh" (AT), refers not to a past coming (as in 1 John 4:2), but to a future one: the elder expects a material, millennial reign of Christ (Strecker 1986; Strecker 1996, 232-36). This is too much to build on the tense of a single verb, however, especially when its context points so strongly to commonality with 1 John (see the commentary).

If 2 John does come from the same historical situation as 1 John, the question arises why it was written at all. Perhaps it was "an initial emergency measure" prior to 1 John (Thomas 1995, 72), or perhaps it was addressed to a congregation in a more distant place, which the opponents' ideas might reach by means of traveling teachers. Either theory would explain the letter's exhortation not to offer the hospitality and base of operations usually afforded such travelers, if they do not bring the appropriate Christology.

# Setting and Purpose of 3 John

With 3 John we seem to come into a different set of issues altogether. There is no mention of false teaching or Christology. Instead, the subject is hospitality in the church (a word used only here in the Johannine writings) and a conflict between the elder and someone named Diotrephes, who had refused this hospitality to the elder's messengers. None of the persons named in 3 John, other than the elder, is known to us from elsewhere. Indeed, were it not for the elder's authorship of 2 John and 2 John's relationship to 1 John, this short note might never have become part of the New Testament, or even been preserved at all (see Lieu 1986, 5-36). Yet the questions it raises about life in the early church offer important material for reflection.

One obvious purpose of 3 John is to encourage Gaius, its recipient, to continue his own hospitality toward Christian travelers. Such hospitality was essential to the functioning of the early Christian mission (see the commentary; for further background, see Lieu 1986, 125-35). Third John is thus, in part, a letter of recommendation for traveling missionaries, and perhaps for Demetrius in particular (v. 12). It is also an exhortation to Gaius to follow good examples, like that of Demetrius, and avoid bad ones, such as Diotrephes. However, Diotrephes is not mentioned simply as a bad example, but is directly connected with the request that the elder makes of Gaius. This is the most difficult problem in 3 John: the nature of the conflict between the elder and Diotrephes, and how this relates to Gaius (see the summary and critique of proposed solutions in Lieu 1986, 149-55; also Brown 1982, 733-38). The significance of the latter must be kept in mind. There is a tendency to focus on the mysterious Diotrephes, and so lose sight of the fact that the person in whom the elder is primarily interested is Gaius.

It is natural to assume that 3 John is related to the doctrinal issues treated in 1 and 2 John, and to make Diotrephes one of the christological opponents (Houlden 1973, 7-8; Bonnard 1983, 135). Yet the elder, who minces no words in the other epistles, does not mention Christology here, or call Diotrephes by any of the terms of disparagement found in 1 and 2 John. Therefore, Ernst Käsemann suggested that the elder, who cannot accuse Diotrephes of heresy, must be a heretic himself; or at least Diotrephes must believe him to be one, because of the radicalism of Johannine theology (Käsemann 1951; Vouga 1990, 17-18). This logic seems to assume that heretics thought of themselves as heretics, however, and implies that Diotrephes was not a Johannine Christian, which is unlikely. If the christological dispute was involved, perhaps the most plausible suggestion is that Diotrephes simply extended the measures of 2 John 10-11 to all traveling teachers, whoever they claimed to represent (Brown 1982, 738; Klauck 1992, 109). The most likely explanation for the silence about this dispute, however, is the most obvious one: 3 John simply has nothing to do with it.

Authority in the church, on the other hand, is mentioned in 3 John in a way that makes it seem new and controversial. Diotrephes has enough power to prevent a letter from the elder from being read to the church, and to expel church members who want to show hospitality to his envoys (though this expulsion need not have been what later came to be called excommunication). Therefore it has long been held that Diotrephes is the first known example of a bishop exercising sole authority over a congregation, an authority in conflict with the older province-wide missionary authority of the elder (Harnack 1897, 20-23). Those who believe that doctrinal issues were involved sometimes suggest that Diotrephes was using his new authority to control doctrine (Schunack 1982, 110). Others propose that the elder himself was already virtually a bishop (Donfried 1977). All this goes well beyond what 3 John actually says, however. The elder can only threaten to "bring up" Diotrephes' actions before the congregation; yet he can hope that this mere oral protest, on Diotrephes' home territory, will succeed. There is clearly no unchallengeable authority on either side. In fact, that is part of the problem. Diotrephes may have been the host of a church that met at his house, in a situation where the "official" status of such hosts was ambiguous. Power, rather than authority, would have been the issue in his refusal of hospitality to the elder's messengers (Malherbe 1983, 96-100, 106-10). A further factor would have been honor, an important value in ancient Mediterranean society. Diotrephes' refusal of the elder's request for hospitality would have been a public challenge to his honor, requiring a response (Malina 1986, 187).

Diotrephes' exact motives are unclear, and they may always remain so, since we have only the elder's viewpoint. Diotrephes' actions would have hindered the elder's mission work, but we do not know whether that was his aim or merely a by-product of a personal power struggle. The Johannine tradition was fundamentally egalitarian, without official structures (see below on the church in the epistles). Because power and authority had arisen in the community without theological justification or interpretation, both the elder and Diotrephes may have found themselves in an ambiguous situation (Lieu 1986, 156-59). Third John presents us with a conflict involving both hospitality (and therefore honor and mission) and power; but its exact dimensions and causes are obscure to us, and may have been so even to its protagonists.

Gaius must have lived in the same town or vicinity as Diotrephes, but he cannot have been a member of Diotrephes' church, since the elder has to inform him of the latter's actions. Yet because the elder calls Diotrephes' congregation "*the* church" (v. 9), it is unlikely that Gaius belonged to some other house-church. Conceivably he headed a Christian household large enough that, while it was not a "church," its members held their own worship meetings and did not belong to any other congregation. The elder writes as if he has a close and confident relationship with Gaius, who had previously shown hospitality to travelers associated with him, the "brothers and sisters" of verses 3, 5, 10 (NRSV: "friends"). It is not clear whether this hospitality was on the same occasion as Diotrephes' rejection of them, or whether their mission now (vv. 5-8) is the same as then. Instead of bearing a letter to "the church," they are now on mission for "the Name" (AT), and Gaius is asked not only to receive them, which Diotrephes refused to do, but to "send them on," that is, supply their needs for the next stage of their journey. Nothing indicates that the elder is seeking Gaius's assistance against Diotrephes, with whom he plans to deal personally. On the whole, regardless of how Diotrephes may have conceived matters, the elder seems to be more annoyed with him than involved in a life-and-death struggle. With Gaius's help, the elder can work around him. It may be wise not to exaggerate the seriousness of the problem, and to content ourselves with the meager information that 3 John provides.

## Dates and Location

If 1 and 2 John are addressed to the same situation, then they must have been written about the same time. Since nothing clearly connects 3 John to the conflicts behind the other two, it could easily have been written a few years earlier (Thomas 1995) or a few years later than they. Its similarity to 2 John in form indicates only common authorship, not nearness of date. Its seemingly more developed (or at least less distinctively Johannine) sense of church and mission may suggest that it is the latest of the epistles, but even this is far from certain.

Absolute dates for these texts can be determined only within a broad range. First John probably represents developments in the Johannine community after the writing of the Fourth Gospel, but it is impossible to know exactly how much time has passed. If the Gospel is dated sometime in the 90s of the first century, then 1 and 2 John could have been written in the first decade of the second century, prior to the rise of the Docetists and Cerinthus discussed above. At any rate there seems no reason to think of their being written later than about 115. If 1 John 4:2-3 and/or 2 John 7 is quoted by Polycarp (Poly. *Phil.* 7.1), that would confirm this general dating.

As to location, the tradition of the church has always placed the Johannine writings in Ephesus. Nothing in the epistles strongly confirms or contradicts this, though the early knowledge of them in Asia Minor does support it. It should be noted that the references to traveling in 2 and 3 John suggest that the communities addressed were not all in the same location, though they must have been fairly near one another.

## LITERARY CHARACTERISTICS

The two small epistles are relatively easy to classify and understand in literary terms. First John presents two serious problems, however. The first concerns the kind of writing that it is, and the second its structure and the development of its argument.

### 1 John

Whatever 1 John may be, it is not a letter. To be sure, like a letter it was written by a particular author to a particular group in regard to a particular situation. But it lacks the formal characteristics of an ancient letter: the names of author and recipient at the beginning, and opening and closing greetings such as are found in 2 and 3 John. Granted this, scholars have sought instead to classify it as an essay or sermon or enchiridion or church order (e.g., Marshall

1978, 99; Smalley 1984, xxxiii; Grayston 1984, 3-4; Hills 1991). None of these quite catches its character, however. First John envisions a specific situation, and is intended to persuade the readers to maintain traditional values rather than accept the innovations of the opponents. Thus, though it may not have the expected development and structure (see below), it bears some of the marks of ancient demonstrative (epideictic) rhetoric, including its typically Johannine stating and restating of basic precepts (Watson 1989a, 1993).

First John may also be considered exhortation (parenesis) done in Johannine style. Its persuasive methods are not only rational but rhetorical and emotional. Antitheses (1:6–2:1; 2:4-11; 3:4-10) and general statements ("everyone who . . . "; 2:23, 29; 3:3-10, 15; 4:7; 5:1, 4, 18 [variously translated in the NRSV]) firmly characterize the two sides in the conflict. Discernment formulas ("by this we know . . . " [AT]; see the comments on 2:3) furnish the tests to determine who is truly in relationship with God. The author also uses many of the techniques of exhortation common in antiquity. There are fixed, well-known formulations and slogans (2:12-14); examples for imitation, especially Jesus and God (2:6; 3:3-16; 4:7-11); and assurances of the wisdom, goodness, and competence of the readers, who need only to be reminded of what they already know (2:12-14, 21, 27). Such parenetic techniques account for much of the tone of reassurance in 1 John. The author tries to draw the readers onto his side in more subtle ways as well. Simple use of pronouns such as "we," "you," and "they" often intimates that the readers are already in agreement with him (1:5–2:2; 4:4-6). The final statement of purpose in 5:13 assumes that the readers share the author's Christology and so possess eternal life.

The structure of 1 John is every bit as hard to specify as its genre (see Brown 1982, 116-23, 764; Segovia 1987, 133-34). Some parts of it seem carefully designed, for example, 1:5–2:11, and the way that 3:23-24 introduces 4:1-18. Yet there is no obvious overall outline, and efforts to find a tight literary structure generally prove artificial and unconvincing (e.g., Smalley 1984, xxxiii-xxxiv; Malatesta 1978, especially 39-40). It is probably too extreme in the other direction, though, to see it as simply "a tract made up of self-contained sections" (O'Neill 1966, 2). One intriguing possibility is that 1 John is patterned structurally after the Gospel of John (Feuillet 1972; Brown 1982, 124-28). Beyond the beginnings and endings, however, the similarity between the two breaks down (see the literary analysis of 3:11-17).

Some scholars have sought to explain 1 John's uneven and difficult surface as resulting from the editing of a source, whether pre-Christian Gnostic (Bultmann 1967a), Jewish sectarian (O'Neill 1966), or Johannine traditional (Grayston 1984, 3-5). Few commentators have found such theories convincing, however (see the critiques of Bultmann in Piper 1947, 447-51; Braun 1951, 264-70; Nauck 1957, 68-83; Wengst 1978, 21-24). First John is an occasional writing from beginning to end, written with a single purpose in view, even if this purpose is not always clearly expressed or achieved. The one passage most easily regarded as a secondary addition may be 5:14-21, since 5:13 seems an appropriate ending to the text, and what follows is rather miscellaneous. Yet even here it is easier to show connections to the rest of 1 John than to say what circumstances could have called forth this "addition" (Nauck 1957, 134-46).

Such progression of thought as 1 John does have cannot really be represented in a comprehensive outline. Important themes recur constantly; if there is a climax anywhere, it is in 4:7-18, with its assertion that the God who is love has been revealed in Jesus Christ. But the various themes appear at too many points and in too many combinations to speak of development, or of divisions and subdivisions. Even the figure of a spiral, implying the return or alternation of themes at progressively higher levels (Law 1914, 5; Houlden 1973, 22-24), does not quite do justice to 1 John's unstructured sequence. Instead, we should bear in mind the essential message of 1 John, that relationship with God requires both incarnational Christology and mutual love, and that these two are inseparably united. It would be fully in character for this author to construct a text in which themes combine and units blend, precisely as a way of enacting this unity. (It is also in character that this aim is not always perfectly carried out, producing ambiguity and rough transitions rather than textual unity.) It has been suggested that the structure of 1 John reflects the author's experience of Christianity (Feuillet 1972, 325-27; Malatesta 1978, 38-39, 194). This is essentially correct, but it would be better to say that the *lack* of structure in the text, its virtual indivisibility, reflects the author's experience of Christianity as one undifferentiated life of faith in Jesus Christ and love for one another.

It may be more fruitful exegetically, then, to examine the smaller sections and units of 1 John, and the interrelations among them, than to provide an overall outline. This is done in detail in the commentary, for the purposes of which I divide the text into thirteen sections, as seen in the table of contents. (In this division I find myself in close agreement with Marshall 1978, 26; Bonnard 1983, 145; and Johnson 1993, v.) For the sake of convenience, I have divided one long segment into two on formal grounds (1:5–2:2; 2:3-11) and combined two discrete units into one (2:12-17). Structural boundaries are often hard to determine because of the presence of transitional elements of the kind that Brown calls "hinges" (1982, 119). A hinge shares to some extent in both of two adjacent parts, making it difficult, and to some extent arbitrary, to assign it to one or the other. See, for example, the literary analyses of 3:18-24 and 4:19–5:5.

## 2 John

For the structures of 2 and 3 John in relation to the conventions of ancient letters, see their respective literary analyses in the commentary. It has been proposed that 2 John is a fabrication created by combining the form of 3 John with the content of 1 John (Bultmann 1973, 107-15; Heise 1967, 164-70), but this is most unlikely. Second John is simply too slight to be worth the effort of such an artifice. Judith Lieu suggests that it is a contrived attempt by the author of 3 John to write in the Johannine style, while using the format of the "apostolic" letter created by Paul, with the aim of increasing his authority and his Johannine standing, in order to deliver, not directives against specific heretics, but a generalized warning based on 1 John (1986, *passim*). There is some merit in this. Second John does seem intended to be a more official and authoritative letter than 3 John. But it is hardly likely, given his evident position in the Johannine community, that the elder was not an authentic participant in its tradition and language. Moreover, openness to Pauline and other non-Johannine language is present already in 1 John. Rather, 2 John is to be understood as what it seems to be, a genuine parenetic letter exhorting the readers to take specific action against known opponents. The writer's relationship with the readers, the resemblance to early Christian official letters, and the rhetoric used (Watson 1989b) all suggest that it is intended to be an authoritative but not coercive exhortation.

## 3 John

The genre of 3 John is not in any doubt (Lieu 1986, 37-51). It is a typical private letter, closer to the common Greek pattern than any other early Christian writing. It differs only in lacking both the usual opening *chairein*, "Greetings," and a standard closing salutation, for which it substitutes "Peace to you." These differences may be meant to indicate the author's personal authority. The great similarity of its ending to that of 2 John seems to represent the elder's individual style.

Third John has only a relatively small amount of distinctively Johannine language, and what there is tends to be used formally or even in slogans. In its place, the conventions of ancient letters of recommendation and the ecclesiastical and mission terminology of the early church dominate the epistle. Like 1 and 2 John, 3 John also shows features typical of parenesis, particularly in the praise of Gaius in verses 1-6, and in verses 9-12, where the elder presents Gaius with a good example to follow and a bad one to avoid. All this need not imply that such usages, rather than the Johannine idiom, reflect the elder's native habits (Lieu 1986, 164). It was, rather, the occasion itself that called for the use of private-letter conventions, parenesis, and the language of mission.

## THEOLOGICAL ISSUES

The two most obvious areas of theological interest in the Johannine epistles are usually summed up as Christology and ethics, and

the christological issue is generally assumed to be the more fundamental. In 1 John 3:23, for example, we find first the commandment to believe in Jesus and then the commandment to love one
another. There are two problems with this approach, however. One
is that the epistles are not concerned with "ethics." First John does
speak of sin and righteousness, but gives hardly any details about
what they are. The only ethical category of interest to the author is
love for one another, and love rather than "ethics" seems the more
appropriate heading. The other problem concerns the relation
between love and Christology. The assumption that christological
issues have priority is not easily justified from 1 John, which gives
much more space to love; it seems instead to derive from a theological paradigm in which matters of faith always have precedence
over matters of action. First John, however, joins Christology and
love firmly together, without giving either priority over the other,
as is already clear in 1 John 3:23 and becomes even clearer in
4:7-18. This interrelationship must be understood before either
theme can be considered.

God's act of love in the incarnation of Christ is absolutely prior
to any human response. Yet neither correct faith nor mutual love
has complete priority as a response to this act. Indeed, the two of
them together are one single response. Christology is the first topic
that 1 John addresses (1:1-4), but this in no way implies that
Christology could be fully understood before ever turning to love.
The language of 3:11 suggests that the message of salvation in Jesus
Christ and the message that Christians are to love one another are
the same message: *love is not law but gospel.* In Jesus was revealed
not only the God who is love, but the good news that human beings
can love one another with this same love. Love is a response of faith,
*the* response of faith, to the revelation of God in Jesus Christ; faith
is faith in *Jesus* only to the extent that it is also love for one another
(Wengst 1976, 74-79). The incarnational Christology of 1 John has
no sense and is not complete without the ethic of love, just as this
love has no foothold and no rationale without the coming of Jesus
the Messiah in human flesh. Thus, though Christology and love
will follow sequentially below, in reality the discussion of each must
incorporate the other.

# Christology

Both 1 and 2 John were written as responses to a specific conflict (3 John mentions Jesus only indirectly, in v. 7), but the dialogue with the opponents led the elder to articulate and interpret the Johannine christological tradition in ways that are meaningful beyond this conflict. Like the Gospel of John itself, 1 John presents a solution greater than the problem to which it was addressed.

The confession of Jesus as the divine Christ and Son of God who has come in human flesh is central to the epistles (1 John 2:22-23; 3:23–4:3; 4:15; 5:1, 5-13, 20; 2 John 3, 7, 9). Not only his divinity but his humanity as such, especially his death by oppressive violence, has lasting significance for salvation and for the knowledge of God. This Christology is endorsed by the very testimony of God, who abides in those who confess it and has given them the Spirit and eternal life. It has never been easy for Christians to hold this paradoxical belief clearly and in all its fullness. The tendency is to neglect one aspect or the other, to see either the all-powerful Redeemer or the humble teacher, rather than seeing what the Johannine writings see, the God of creation revealed in a mortal man, revealed in his mortality itself.

This Christology is never presented in isolation, however, but is always connected to issues of salvation and mutual love. Most of the roles that Christians have historically seen in Jesus are present in 1 John. He is the Savior, the atoning sacrifice for sins, and stands as our intercessor with God (2:1-2; 4:9-10, 14). He is also the one who makes God known as love, and reveals God's love as self-giving and compassionate (4:7-10, 14-16; 5:20). The relationship Christians have with God results from this work of Jesus as Savior and revealer. Yet his role as mediator of their communion with God is mostly implicit; indeed, it is reduced from what we find in the Gospel of John (see below). Nor does he appear in the role of teacher, as the giver of the love commandment; 1 and 2 John consistently present this as God's commandment. Jesus' role as an example of love to be imitated is essential, however.

It is important to grasp this broad range of significance given to incarnational Christology. The epistles' insistence on confessing certain statements about Jesus can easily be mistaken for a creedal formalism, a set of test phrases for mechanically determining right belief. What counts, however, is not the formulas but the truth they represent, the Johannine message of the incarnate Jesus Christ. "Jesus Christ has come in the flesh" is not simply a dogma that must be given intellectual assent, but an offer and a call to lead a life freed from sin and permeated by love for one another, to "run the risk of justice" (Morgen 1987, 68). In opposing a Christology that devalued the humanity of Christ, 1 John promoted one that would reshape the lives of believers in all their own human reality.

## Love One Another

This reshaping is actually the first theme treated extensively in 1 John (1:5–2:17). The centrality of love can be seen in the things for which it is the signal and test: knowing and abiding in God (2:3-6; 3:23-24; 4:7-8, 12, 16), walking in the light (2:9-11), being God's child (2:29; 3:10; 4:7), eternal life (3:14), confidence at the judgment (4:17-18), and our own love for God (4:20–5:1). People do not become children of God by their own good deeds; to be born of God is a gift of God's love, which calls forth and enables Christians' love (3:1-2; 4:9-11, 19). Yet love united to christological confession is the one unfailing test of those who truly are God's children (4:7; 5:1). Where there is no love at work, there is no Christianity. This implies that Christianity is not purely a matter of individual salvation, since love cannot be practiced by one person alone. Knowing God, loving God, being confident of eternal life— all the things that we might consider "spiritual"—are real only in concrete living in community with other human beings. "Beloved, let us love one another" (4:7).

This way of putting it, though, raises a crucial problem. The Johannine love commandment is specifically "love *one another.*" There is no avoiding the dilemma created by this typically sectarian limitation of love to other members of the community. The open inclusiveness of Jesus' teaching, his love even for enemies, the church's mission to the world, and the very universality of God are all called into question. The danger becomes painfully evident not only in the polemics of 1 John 2:18-23; 4:1-6, but even more sharply in the conflicts of 2 and 3 John. The epistles have been legitimately criticized on this score (Rese 1985, 47-48, 51-58; Klauck 1988, 58, 61-64).

Yet the love they promote is not without positive value. The love commandment is the "new commandment" (1 John 2:8; John 13:34) because it is eschatological, part of the new age begun with the coming of the Messiah. Focusing on love within the Christian community makes this new, eschatological community the concrete sign that the Messiah has come in the human Jesus, in whom the revelation of God as love has been given. The unbreakable unity of love and christological faith in 1 John is one reason why love is active precisely among those who hold this faith. Love for one another thus not only actualizes God's presence within the community, but is essential to the community's mission of making the presence and love of God real and known to the world (John 13:35; 17:20-23). In Johannine sectarianism, moreover, mutual love provides the internal solidarity necessary to defend the community's identity against a hostile world and, in the case of 1 and 2 John, against division within.

Because love for one another is grounded in Jesus, one of the strongest ethical themes in 1 John is the imitation of Jesus (2:6; 3:2-7, 16; 4:17), and even of God (1:5-7; 3:1, 9-10; 4:11, 19; perhaps also 2:29). The call for God's people to be like God is as old as Lev 19:2, and was part of the teaching of Jesus (Luke 6:35-36). In the Gospel of John, imitation is hierarchical: Christians are to imitate Jesus' love for them, which in turn is rooted in God's love for him (John 13:13-17, 34-35; 15:9-13). In 1 John, Christians imitate God directly; but even this has a christological basis, since the God who is love has been made known in Jesus (4:9-11, 14-16). This imitation is not a mechanical conformity but a loving response to the love of God abiding within. Yet it is also as concrete as possible, a matter of visible actions and not only interior feelings (3:17-18), "a self-determination to do good, good only, and always the highest good possible" (Law 1914, 77).

It was Jesus' death for our sake that made known the depth and the nature of divine love (3:16; 4:10), and so it is this in particular that the readers of 1 John are urged to imitate. Only by giving up one's life in love for others can one truly enter life (3:14): in this 1 John expresses the heart of the Christian ethical tradition, which goes back to Jesus himself. Incarnational Christology is essential for Christian ethics, which are not simply an adaptation of the prevalent social code but the result of a divine intrusion into human affairs. This intrusion cost the Son of God his life, and his sacrifice set the standard for the core value of Christian behavior. Christian love thus continues the revelation of God that began in Jesus; in it the love that God is reaches its intended goal (4:12).

## God in the Epistles

The two most notable theological assertions in 1 John are that God is light (1:5) and that God is love (4:8, 16). These statements are essentially equivalent, since "light" in 1 John is not so much a cosmic or intellectual symbol as an ethical one (2:9-11). The author thus expresses an understanding of God that is fundamentally ethical, and fully integrated with his Christology. The invisible God, whom no eye can see and no image represent, has been made known to us as self-giving love by Jesus Christ (4:9-10, 14-16; 5:20), and remains present and in a sense visible to us in our love for one another (4:7-8, 12, 16; 3 John 11). "God is love" is less an abstract statement about what God is than an assertion about what God has done and continues to do. That God is just is therefore not a threat of punishment but a promise of forgiveness (1:9); that God knows everything is not a warning but a reassurance for those whose own consciences accuse them (3:19-20).

One remarkable feature of the epistles is the number of things that they attribute to God that the Gospel of John attributes to Jesus. These include being light (John 1:3b-9; 8:12; 9:4-5; 12:35-36, 46; 1 John 1:5) and giving the love commandment (John 13:34; 15:10, 12, 17; 1 John 2:3-11; 3:22-24; 4:21; 5:2-3; 2 John 4-6). Instead of abiding in Jesus as Jesus abides in God (John 14:20; 15:4-10; 17:21-23), Christians abide directly in God (1 John 2:5-6; 3:24; 4:12-16; 5:20). Instead of praying in Jesus' name or while abiding in him (John 14:13-14; 15:7, 16; 16:23-27), they are confident in prayer because they keep God's commandments or ask according to God's will (1 John 3:22; 5:14-15). Overall, Jesus' role as mediator between Christians and God is reduced. Relationship with Jesus and mediation by him are not eliminated (1 John 1:3; 2:1, 23-24; 5:11-12, 20), but the epistles seem to focus primarily on their result, the direct relationship between Christians and God. This shift of focus seems important, but the reason for it is unclear. The author may stress God, whose role is undisputed, because the opponents had cast doubt on the role of Jesus (von Wahlde 1990, 204-5). Or this may simply be part of 1 John's general affinity for non-Johannine Christianity, which does not emphasize the hierarchical relationship from God to Jesus to Christians as much as the Fourth Gospel does.

## Other Theological Topics

The epistles touch on a variety of theological issues, including sin, eschatology, and the Spirit. The church and its life are especially prominent in 2 and 3 John, and the role of tradition is important in different ways in all three epistles. Several of these issues are affected by the dualism that runs throughout 1 John and is present in the smaller epistles as well.

### Dualism

In 1 John there are sharp oppositions between light and darkness; love and hate; truth and falsehood or deception; and God or Christ and the evil one or the antichrist. The opponents and their ways are identified with the negative poles of each of these contrasts. The world itself is opposed to God and is in the power of the evil one (2:15-17; 5:19), though Jesus remains its Savior (2:2; 4:14). This is not quite the same as the cosmic dualism of some forms of Gnosticism, which divides the world into two opposing natures that control spiritual destiny. Instead, its ethical and eschatological aspects bring this dualism closer to Jewish apocalyptic texts and the Qumran writings. Like the latter in particular, the epistles' dualism is strongly colored by the sectarianism of the community. The sense of alienation from a hostile and uncomprehending world is one part of their Johannine heritage that the epistles not only preserve but strengthen. It is this world whose conquest 1 John reaffirms (4:4-6; 5:4-5), the world that hates God's children because it has never known God (3:1, 13), not the natural world created by God.

## Salvation and Sin

First John comes close to a deterministic conception of salvation, in asserting that children of God and of the devil are irrevocably distinct from one another and are known absolutely by their conduct (3:4-10; 5:18). Yet these statements are contradicted by others that insist that even Christians can sin (1:5–2:2; 5:16-17). The apparent determinism is also relieved by the fact that 1 John does not actually say that anyone is born of the devil and therefore predestined to sin. In fact it says almost nothing about how one *becomes* a child of God or of the devil, which also leaves it unclear whether a person can change from one category to the other (note 2:19). The author is not interested in the nature of such origins but in the behaviors that make the origins plain. The author may have borrowed the deterministic language from his opponents; yet it is so tightly integrated into the epistle that he apparently found it an acceptable means of expressing the sharp contrast he saw between the true way and that of the opponents.

This still leaves the question of whether Christians can or cannot sin. The author's overriding concern is that the readers, who had not yet gone over to the opponents, should not sin (2:1). To this end, he affirmed both the possibility of sinlessness in acts of love and the possibility of failure, along with the certainty of divine forgiveness. God's true children, unlike the opponents, love one another; sin and hatred are part of the old world overcome by Christ and now passing away (2:8-9, 17; 3:5, 8; 5:3-5). Yet this is not an automatic process. The readers must be exhorted to continue living in love, and must be assured of forgiveness if they do sin. Something like this, at any rate, seems to be the point of the troublesome contradictions about sin in 1 John.

## Eschatology

The Gospel of John is well known for its characteristic "realized eschatology," that is, its assertion that future eschatological events such as resurrection, judgment, and eternal life are already present for those who believe (e.g., John 4:25-26; 5:24-25; 11:25). The same pattern appears in 1 John 2:8; 3:14; 5:12, and in the claim that the antichrist and the last hour are already present (1 John 2:18, 22; 4:1-3; 2 John 7). However, we also find the orientation toward Christ's *future* coming and the last judgment that are common elsewhere in early Christianity (1 John 2:28–3:3; 4:17-18). Yet even these passages emphasize the present condition of believers as children of God who are like Jesus (3:1-3; 4:17), and there is no indication that eschatology itself was an issue in the conflict. The most prominent eschatological conception in 1 John is eternal life. Though it can be thought of as a promise for the future (2:25), those who love one another and believe in Jesus have eternal life already (3:14-15; 5:11-13). While 1 John characteristically says that God, rather than Jesus, is eternal life (5:20), it is Jesus who has made God known, so that in the incarnate Christ the life that was with God appeared (1:1-2). Eternal life can thus be spoken of with reference to past, present, and future, but the main emphasis remains on the presence of life now, made possible by the coming of the Son of God.

## The Church

Of all the Johannine writings, only 3 John uses the word "church." Second John uses the unusual terminology of the "elect lady" and her "elect sister" to refer to Christian congregations, which may express a sense of the church's divine calling (Lieu 1986, 67); but the letter says nothing further about this. Otherwise, though all three epistles plainly show the marks of a communal history, the only term they have for the community is *adelphoi*, "brothers and sisters," used seventeen times to refer to other Christians. The metaphor of Christians as a family of God's children is thus their primary way of speaking about the church (Rusam 1993, 163-65, 185-86). The Johannine tradition was an egalitarian one, without hierarchy or offices, instead emphasizing unity, mutual love, and access to the Spirit (John 13:34-35; 14:26; 15:12-13, 17; 16:12-15; 17:11, 20-26; 20:21-23; see Klauck 1989). The epistles display something of both the positive and negative potential of such an approach. As noted above, they also display the sectarian perception of the community as set apart from the world, a perception already present in the Fourth Gospel, and now intensified by the schism that had broken the community's fellowship.

Both 2 and 3 John show that the house-churches and the traveling teachers, missionaries, and messengers familiar from elsewhere in the New Testament were present in Johannine Christianity, at least at this stage. But there is no theology of the church in the epistles; indeed, this lack of reflection may itself be partly responsible for the problems they address. In 1 John, the author does not invoke any sort of structural authority against the opponents, no title or rank or organizational means of imposing his interpretation. The only uncontested "authority" is that of witness (1:1-4; 4:14). Even in 2 John, the measures of control are not clearly *institutional,* and the elder offers no sanctions to enforce his exhortation. In 3 John, likewise, whether or not Diotrephes is seeking a more structured authority, the elder has nothing to use against him but words. In both 2 and 3 John, the issues still seem to revolve around individuals rather than structures or regulations.

What remains essential is the community itself (Lieu 1991, 70-71, 105-10; Lieu 1986, 143-54). The community continues the Johannine witness, and in the exercise of love among its members it is the ongoing revelation of God. These members know the truth (1 John 2:21), and can carry out the tests that 1 John proposes. By prayer, they see to one another's restoration from sins (5:16). In 2 and 3 John we see this egalitarian sense of communal responsibility under greater stress. But on the whole the epistles maintain the Johannine understanding of the church, as sheep with one Shepherd and branches of a single Vine, united by love for one another and so bearing witness to the coming of God's Messiah.

## Tradition and Spirit

In keeping with this egalitarianism, all Johannine Christians have the anointing of the Spirit and need no human teacher (1 John

2:20-21, 27). Yet the leading of the Spirit itself has become problematic, and needs to be tested (4:1-6). The criterion proposed in 1 John for validating claims of inspiration is continuity with the Johannine christological tradition "from the beginning" (2:22-24). The Spirit has testified to the blood of the crucified Jesus in the Johannine tradition and gospel, and therefore is present now only where the humanity of the incarnate Christ is affirmed (5:6-8).

This appeal to tradition creates the risk that no new ideas, no "going forward" (2 John 9 [AT]), will be tolerated at all. Some have seen in 1 John an incipient "rule of faith," a dogmatic standard against which all teaching must be judged (see the concluding comments on 5:6-12). But 1 John presents a distinctively *Johannine* approach to tradition, a dynamic relationship between tradition and Spirit. The tradition is valid only because it is the testimony of the Spirit of truth. The author himself interprets, reformulates, and adapts the Johannine tradition in many ways, and submits his exhortation to abide in the tradition to the judgment of the anointed community. The word *tradition* itself is not used, nor are there institutional safeguards to preserve tradition. Instead, the emphasis is on the word, commandment, truth, or testimony itself, and above all on its *content*. The tradition claims that in the person of Jesus Christ the truth of the God who is love was revealed, and therefore it resists any attempt to know God apart from the flesh of Jesus and love for one another. The author will affirm neither spirit nor tradition unless it confesses this indispensable truth: God is love, and was revealed among us in the sending of Jesus Christ, so that through his sacrifice we might live and love one another.

# COMMENTARY: 1 JOHN

## PROLOGUE (1:1-4)

Like the Gospel of John, 1 John begins with a prologue. In fact, many of its terms (including "the beginning," "the word" [Gk. *logos*], "life," "testify," "the Father," and the "Son") echo the Gospel's prologue. Some of these expressions are found throughout John, and others are at least distinctively Johannine: what we have heard and seen (John 3:32); and complete joy (John 3:29; 15:11; 16:24; 17:13). The prologue thus seems deliberately intended to plunge the reader into the Johannine world of language and thought, whether or not its author is also the author of the Gospel.

To grasp the structure of the prologue one must contend with its nearly impossible grammar. The first verse actually consists only of a series of relative clauses and a prepositional phrase standing in a kind of apposition to them. The Greek reader expects eventually to find a verb governing all these relative clauses, and that verb can only be "we declare" in verse 3. (Hence some English translations, including the NRSV, insert another "we declare to you" in v. 1.) Verse 2 is really an interruption explaining "the word of life." Verse 3 then resumes verse 1, finally delivering the main verb. But that is not quite all, for the "interruption" in verse 2 repeats "life" and "we have seen" from verse 1, and also introduces "we declare" and "the Father," which will appear in verse 3. Thus, verse 2 is not merely an interruption but a bridge between verses 1 and 3, and verse 3 summarizes both of the first two verses before moving onward. This is underscored by the repetition of "revealed" in an inclusion that ties together the beginning and the end of verse 2.

Though the result is grammatically poor and literarily awkward, this all seems quite deliberate. It succeeds in conducting the reader from the events of the past, when "the life" was revealed, to the present testimony of the author who is in fellowship both with the readers and with God. The placement of "his Son Jesus Christ" at the end of verse 3 both dramatically introduces by name the one who has been the subject all along, and sonorously rounds off the whole construction. Verse 4, however, is thereby left somewhat dangling.

◊ ◊ ◊ ◊

The deliberate echoes of the prologue to the Fourth Gospel may be meant to begin the author's critique of the interpretation of Johannine tradition put forward by the opponents. The Gospel's insistence on the divinity and preexistence of the one who came into the world would have supported the opponents' Christology very well. The author thus starts by attacking these opponents on what may have been some of their own favorite ground.

"What was from the beginning" (v. 1) is an obvious allusion to John 1:1, which itself alludes to Gen 1:1. There are some significant changes, however. First John uses a neuter pronoun ("what") instead of masculine ("who"), and says "*from* the beginning" rather than "*in* the beginning." In the Gospel "the beginning" clearly refers to the beginning of all things. Here, however, it seems to mean the beginning of the Christian tradition in the revelation of Jesus. The neuter pronoun, the incarnational language, and the absence of reference to the creation all suggest this, as does a comparison with the other instances of things heard "from the beginning" in these epistles (1 John 2:7, 24; 3:11; 2 John 5-6). First John is not concerned with the existence of the divine Word *in* the beginning, but with the persistence of the true message, "the word of life," *since* the beginning (see John 5:24; 6:63, 68; 8:51). Nevertheless, the allusion to the Gospel prologue inevitably reminds the reader of the absolute beginning, and it is clear from verses 2-3 that the subject of the message is the eternal divine life incarnate.

The emphasis on sense perception in verse 1, however, climaxing in "touched," recalls the physical human reality that was also part of the Johannine tradition "from the beginning." It underscores a central aspect of 1 John's message, that Jesus Christ truly came "in the flesh" (4:2; 2 John 7), that he was a real human being, not just a divine spirit, a reality that the opponents downplayed. In another classically Johannine formulation in verse 2, we learn that it was life itself, which had been in God's presence (see John 1:1), that was revealed in Jesus. This manifestation of life corresponds to the incarnation of the Logos in John 1:14. However, the author has again modified the Johannine terms. The Gospel of John never uses "life" in this fashion as virtually a title for Jesus, nor does it call the incarnation itself the "revelation" of the incarnate Christ (see also 1 John 3:5, 8; contrast John 1:31; 2:11; 7:4; 21:1, 14; usages similar to 1 John are found in 1 Tim 3:16; Heb 9:26; 1 Pet 1:20). By so closely identifying life with the incarnate one in whom it was revealed, 1 John underlines the need for a faith that takes in the full humanity of Jesus in order to receive the gift of eternal life (see also 2:22-25; 5:11-13). The result is a fully incarnational conception: the divine life was revealed in a visible and tangible person who was witnessed, and this revelation itself is embodied in the message that has been handed on since that beginning.

The stress on physical knowledge in verse 1 is often taken as evidence that 1 John was written by someone who knew Jesus himself. But the probable date of 1 John works against this; in any case, the text here is intended to give testimony, not to report the author's eyewitness status. The notion of testimony to what has been seen (see also 4:14) emphasizes the author's place in the Johannine tradition, indeed in a tradition stretching all the way back to John the Baptist (John 1:32-34; 3:11; 19:35). The use of the first-person plural in the prologue is related to this sense of being part of a corporate tradition. The Greek syntax in verse 3 can best be rendered "we declare *in turn* to you": the author, or the group that he represents, is a link in a chain of testimony extending from the events of the revelation of eternal life in Jesus to the readers of 1 John. This continuous witness to the message of the revelation authenticates the author's interpretation of that message for the readers.

The ordinary sense of the word "fellowship" *(koinōnia)* is sharing or partnership, a usage that may have been common in the early Christian mission (see the comments on 2 John 11). Here it seems to correspond to the language of mutual indwelling with God and with Christ that is common in John and elsewhere in 1 John (see the comments on 2:6), though it suggests more strongly the importance of a *community*. Since the word is totally absent from John, its appearance four times in 1 John 1:3-7 is noteworthy. The application of fellowship language to God, which occurs only here in the entire Bible (although it is common in Greek thought), may have originated with the opponents (v. 6). If that is the case, then the author's invitation to fellowship implies an invitation away from them. By putting themselves outside the tradition of witness to the incarnation, thus separating themselves from the light of love, the opponents have cut themselves off from the partnership of the Johannine community and from fellowship with God. The opponents are probably also in view when the author speaks of God's "Son Jesus Christ," since a significant element in his christological message is that Jesus *is* the Christ and the Son of God (2:22-24; 3:23; 4:15; 5:1, 5). These titles are deeply rooted in the Johannine tradition (John 11:27; 20:31), but their use here helps to introduce the specific subject of 1 John.

The statement of the author's purpose for writing in verse 4 may be compared with others in 2:1; 5:13. The joy mentioned here is not merely an emotion, but an eschatological blessing (John 15:11; 16:20-24; 17:13). The author's joy, and that of the group he represents, is complete if the readers are included among those who have fellowship with God and Jesus by adhering to the tradition of witness to the incarnation (cf. the role of John the Baptist in John 3:29; contrast 2 John 12). Thus even the author's fellowship with God is not fully satisfactory without the readers' incorporation.

◊ ◊ ◊ ◊

First John begins with an appeal to the Johannine community's tradition, presented in a way that asserts a claim to the correct interpretation of that tradition, over against the innovations of the opponents. Unlike the prologue to the Fourth Gospel, however, the "word of life" that was from the beginning is less the personal Logos in whom life came into existence than the message that offers life to its hearers. In the Johannine tradition, this message is primarily about Jesus. But in 1 John 3:14 life is connected with love of one another, and thus the word of life also includes the commandment of love, which is the message heard from the beginning (2:7-11; 3:11; 2 John 5). It is *this* word, embodied in the human Jesus, that truly gives life.

The readers are linked to this word by the testimony that draws them into fellowship with the author (and the tradition he represents), who in turn is in fellowship with the Father and the Son. This should not be understood as a hierarchy; the readers are not being invited to occupy their place in an institutional diagram. Rather, the author wants to incorporate the readers into the partnership of those who know the life that was revealed, so that the readers may participate with them in their participation with God and with Jesus Christ.

This implies that fellowship with God can really only be gained, not by an independent and individual religious life, but by joining this tradition and its adherents, an implication open both to a fully hierarchical ecclesiastical interpretation and to the Gnostic concept of a secret tradition that must be received for salvation. Both of these are developments beyond what is present in 1 John, however. The prologue should instead be understood in the light of 4:7–5:5: It is those who share in the mutual love of the true Christian community, marked by its continuity with the revelation of God as love in the incarnation of Jesus Christ, who truly love and know God.

## WALKING IN THE LIGHT AND SINNING (1:5–2:2)

The first major section of 1 John begins at 1:5 and continues through 2:11. It is marked off by the references to light and darkness in 1:5-7 and 2:8-11; these terms occur only here in 1 John. A series of six "boasts" or claims gives structure to the section. These boasts are probably based on statements made by the author's opponents, which the author regards as false. The section is subdivided into two smaller parts, 1:5–2:2 and 2:3-11, distinguished by the different forms of the boasts: those in 1:6, 8, 10 all begin with "if we say," while those in 2:4, 6, 9 begin with "whoever says."

In this first part, each boast is characterized in terms of truth and lying, and is countered by another "if" sentence that speaks of how sin may be removed (1:7, 9; 2:1). In the first two of these pairs, the boasts and the antithetical sentences are carefully balanced against each other. This symmetry breaks down in the third pair, where the antithesis is separated from the boast by another sentence, and is only implicitly—rather than directly—opposed to the boast. (Thus 2:1a should be taken as being parenthetical rather than as introducing a new section.) Moreover, while the first boast has a claim countered by an inconsistent action (as in 2:4-5, 9-11), the other two have claims that are impossible in themselves.

Verse 1:5 functions as a transition from the prologue ("message" and "proclaim" have the same Greek root as "declare" in 1:3; note also the references to "we," "you," and "hearing"); it also introduces the first boast unit in 1:6-7. At the end of that unit the topic of sin is introduced, which sets up both of the next two boast units. There is thus a kind of "chaining" from one boast to the next. In spite of this, however, there is no terribly clear progression from boast to boast, although there may be some development from the general to the specific.

◊ ◊ ◊ ◊

Verse 1:5 continues the prologue's theme of the message proclaimed in the tradition, a message evidently first heard from Jesus. "God is light" is an assertion with which virtually everyone in the ancient world—Jew, pagan, and Christian—would have agreed in some form (note Jas 1:17). There is a question, however, as to why someone in the *Johannine* tradition would say this, and would ascribe such a message to Jesus. In the Gospel of John, Jesus identifies himself, not God, as light (John 8:12; 9:5; 12:35, 46; see also 1:4-5; 3:19). This is part of a pattern in 1 John of applying to God language that the Gospel uses about Jesus (see the introduction), but there seems to be a particular point behind it here.

One might, of course, reason that if Jesus is light, then God also is light, since Jesus fully discloses God (John 1:18; 14:7-11). However, 1:5 is parallel to two other passages in 1 John. In 3:11 the message is defined again, but as the love commandment; and in 4:8, 16 the author asserts that God is love. Since walking in the light means loving one another (2:9-11), it seems clear that the message "God is light" is equivalent to both "God is love" and the message of the love commandment. The relation of this to Jesus becomes apparent when we note that divine love was revealed in his sending as an atoning sacrifice (4:9-10, 14-16). Because Jesus revealed that God is love, 1 John can say that the message received from him is, "God is light." (It is probably beyond our author's interests, but of course it is also true that the love and mercy of God did play a central role in the teaching of Jesus.)

The dualism of light and darkness is one of the most typical features of the Johannine writings. Light as a metaphor of God occurs in the Hebrew Scriptures (e.g., Ps 27:1; 80:1-3, 7, 19; Hab 3:3-4), and the contrast with darkness is found both in Judaism (e.g., *T. Levi* 19:1; *1 Enoch* 108:11-15; 1QS 1:9-10; 3:19–4:14; Philo *Somn.* 1.75; Philo *Praem.* 36-40, 45-46) and in other hellenistic religious language (e.g., *Corp. Herm.* 1.4-6; 7.2). Elsewhere in the New Testament we also read that Christians are in the realm of light while others are in darkness (Acts 26:18; Col 1:13; 1 Pet 2:9). The origins of this one-sided use of the metaphor of light obviously lie in the common association of day with safety and night with danger. It must be balanced, however, against the inclusion of darkness also in divine symbolism in the Hebrew Scriptures (e.g., Exod 20:21; Ps 18:9-12; Isa 50:10-11; see Gaba 1995).

"Walking," as used in 1:6, 7 and in 2:6, 11, is a well-known Jewish metaphor for how one lives (e.g., Ps 1:1; 15:2; Rom 6:4; 8:4; 14:15; for walking in the light of God, or, by contrast, walking in darkness, see Job 29:3; Ps 56:13; 82:5; Eccl 2:14; Isa 2:5; 9:2; Eph 5:8; Rev 21:24; and at Qumran 1QS 3:20-21). In the Gospel of John, "walking in darkness" seems to refer to ignorance and lostness (8:12; 11:9-10; 12:35), while here it is ethical. No doubt the author's opponents saw themselves also as "in the light" in Johannine terms. John 3:19-21 may furnish the ground for 1 John's insistence that those who really are in the light are distinguished from those who are in darkness by their deeds, especially since it also speaks of "doing the truth" (AT).

The latter expression occurs in the Hebrew Scriptures (2 Chr 31:20; Neh 9:33), but becomes more frequent in later Jewish religious language (e.g., Tob 4:6; 13:6; *T. Reub.* 6:9; 1QS 1:5; 5:3; 8:2). The general sense is of acting faithfully, or of truth as one of several virtues to be "done." Here, however, one must reckon with the significance of "truth" in Johannine thought and in 1 John specifically. Truth is a central concept throughout the Johannine writings (e.g., John 1:14, 17; 4:23-24; 8:31-32; 14:6; 16:13; 17:17-19; 18:37; 1 John 2:8; 3:18-19; 4:6; 5:20; 2 John 1-4; 3 John 3-4). It means the reality of God, a reality that is eternal but was revealed in Jesus. The contrast between truth and lying, however, is found only once in the Gospel (John 8:44-46), whereas in 1 John it is crucial. Our author is very concerned about lying and liars (cf. 1:10 especially with 5:10; see also 2:4, 21-22, 27; 4:1, 20), and about deceit or error (2:26; 3:7; 4:6). Internal conflicts have torn this community whose tradition was pervaded by the claim to truth. Now truth must be separated from falsehood within the community, and it is this that 1 John sets out to do, by subjecting claims of relationship with God to the test of ethical consistency.

In providing an introduction to the first of the "boasts," 1:5 also prepares the way for one of the central ethical themes in 1 John, the imitation of God (and of Christ; see the comments on 2:6). Those who have fellowship with the God who is light cannot be other than as God is. This explains two seeming inconsistencies in the following verses. First, the author says that God is *in* the light just after saying that God *is* light. He does not mean that light is somehow prior to God. Rather, in order to introduce the theme of imitation, there must be a parallel between our condition and God's. It would be difficult to say that we are light, or that God "walks" in the light. To say that God is in the light provides a somewhat less problematic model for our imitation. Second, the author shifts from fellowship with God to fellowship with one another (1:6, 7). Fellowship with one another may be another way of speaking about love, so that imitating God in light and love brings fellowship both with God and with one another. Fellowship with God is thus not a private relationship but involves joining with others in shared tradition (1:3; see the comments there) and in love. We can walk in the light only when we walk with others whom we can love and with whom we can learn of God.

The Greek form of all the "if" clauses in 1:5–2:2 is that of a general condition, one valid at any time. Moreover, the "we" that is used from 1:6 onward clearly refers, not to the author and other witnesses to the tradition, as in the preceding verses, but to the author and the readers together. By these means, the author generalizes the opponents' claims in order to refute them: it is not only the opponents, but *anyone* who might make such unfounded claims who is in error. By making the refutation a general one, the author makes it seem more self-evident. However, he may also have believed that the readers really were at risk of being caught up in these errors. The use of "we" to identify them with himself not only recognizes this, but is part of a conscious strategy to draw them securely to his side of the conflict. Similarly, the affectionate "little children" (2:1) is used throughout 1 John for the addressees (see also 3 John 4). The only similar use elsewhere in the New Testament is in John 13:33, where Jesus uses it in addressing his disciples. Evidently this was the way teachers addressed disciles in the Johannine community (see the comments on 2:27).

To "have sin" is found only in 1:8 and in John 9:41; 15:22, 24; 19:11 in the New Testament. In John it always refers to people hostile to Jesus, so that the opponents may have held that those who believe in Jesus "do not have sin," that is, do not bear the stigma or the guilt of sinfulness, irrespective of their actions (similarly "we have not sinned" in 1:10). Conceivably they may have believed that the new nature given in Christ is incapable of sin. For the author, such assertions are sheer delusion. Those who make them do not have "the truth," the "word" or revelation of God given in Jesus (see the references for "truth" above, and also John 3:33-34; 8:40-47; 17:8). This is in accord with the broad biblical understanding that no one is without sin (1 Kgs 8:46; Ps 14; 143:2; Eccl 7:20; Mark 10:18; Rom 3:9-26). First John, however, is unique in its explicit treatment of whether, and in what way, Christians can sin. Unfortunately, its statements are also uniquely contradictory, and present perhaps its most difficult problem.

Verse 1:7 already contains a paradox: If we are walking in the light, what sins do we have that need cleansing? What is the difference between saying that we walk in the light and saying that we do not have sin, which 1:8, 10 condemn? The problem becomes more acute in 3:4-10, which quite clearly asserts what 1:8, 10 deny, that Christians do not sin. First John 5:16-18 bluntly juxtaposes the idea that Christians may be redeemed from their sins with an assertion of their sinlessness. Each of these passages will require special consideration. With regard to 1:7, perhaps since "walking in the light" primarily means loving one another (2:9-11), it need not imply absolute sinlessness. Those who love their brothers and sisters remain in the relationship with God (the covenant, though 1 John does not use that term) within which their sins are forgiven through Jesus. We may also look to 2:1, where the author's purpose in writing is given as keeping the readers from sin. To this end he holds up both the ideal of walking in the light and the comfort that those who do sin will find Jesus on their side (see also 3:19-20, and the comments there). It is this pastoral and parenetic purpose that allows (though it hardly resolves) the contradictory statements. The conflict with 3:4-10; 5:18 remains especially difficult. The point of those passages may be that one should be sinless in fact, not only in principle. Verses 1:8, 10 may not be completely incongruous with this if they mean that when sin is committed in fact, it cannot be wished away by an appeal to principle.

The contrast to self-deceptive denial of sin is confession (1:9), meaning the acknowledgment of what really is. Elsewhere in the Johannine writings, the term refers to confessing or denying Jesus (John 1:20; 9:22; 12:42; 1 John 2:23; 4:2-3, 15; 2 John 7). Confession of sin was generally public (Mark 1:5; Acts 19:18; Jas 5:16; *Did.* 4:14; 14:1), and that may well be the case here. The use of the plural "sins" (rather than "sin," as in 1:8) is a reminder that not just an abstract confession of sinfulness but the acknowledgment of specific acts is in mind.

The language in which the assurance of divine forgiveness is expressed seems to be drawn from non-Johannine traditions within early Christianity. God is never called "faithful" *(pistos)* elsewhere in the Johannine writings, and in John "just" *(dikaios)* is used only in 17:25. God is called faithful in the Hebrew Scriptures (Deut 7:9; 32:4; Ps 145:13; Isa 49:7), and in Paul this becomes a kind of proverb (1 Cor 1:9; 10:13; 2 Cor 1:18; 1 Thess 5:24; see also 2 Tim 2:13; Heb 10:23; 11:11; 1 Pet 4:19). Even more central to Paul is God's justice, justification, and righteousness *(dikaiosynē)*. Romans 3:21-26 speaks of the just God justifying believers through the atoning sacrifice of Jesus' blood, much the same language as in our passage. The designation of Jesus as "just" or "righteous" (2:1) is reminiscent of Acts 3:14; 7:52; 22:14. In 1 John 2:28–3:10, the *dikaiosynē* of God or Jesus is a model for Christian imitation. Here it refers to the righteousness of God and Jesus in forgiving when imitation fails. Like Paul, 1 John connects divine justice with forgiveness and mercy rather than with punishment, just as in 3:10 "doing righteousness" is identified with loving one's sisters and brothers.

Christ's death is important for salvation in the Gospel of John (3:14-15; 8:28; 10:14-18; 11:50-52; 12:23-36; 15:12-14); but cleansing and forgiveness of sin in Jesus and his blood (see also 1 John 2:12; 3:5, 8; 4:10; 5:6-8) is comparable only to John 1:29; 20:23. First John's opponents evidently denied not only that Jesus is God's son, but also that his death works salvation (2:22-24; 4:9-10, 15; 5:5-13). Therefore, it is not surprising that the author emphasizes these things here, giving a major role to what is at most a muted theme in the Fourth Gospel (so muted that many scholars regard John 6:51-58; 19:34 as redactional). The forgiveness of sins, though found elsewhere in the New Testament (e.g., Matt 6:12-15; Mark 3:28-29; 11:25; Eph 4:32; Col 1:14; Jas 5:15), is a particular specialty of Luke–Acts (e.g., Luke 1:77; 7:47-49; 23:34; 24:47; Acts 2:38; 10:43; 26:18). Cleansing appears in Eph 5:25-27; Titus 2:14; Heb 1:3. Redemption in Jesus' blood is found both in Paul's letters and elsewhere in the New Testament (e.g., Acts 20:28; Rom 5:9; Col 1:20; Heb 10:19; 1 Pet 1:18-19; Rev 5:9), and the *combination* of Jesus' blood specifically with cleansing or forgiveness of sins occurs in Matt 26:28; Eph 1:7; Heb 9:12-14; and Rev 1:5. The expression "atoning sacrifice" *(hilasmos)* is also not Johannine. It occurs only here (2:2) and at 4:10 in the New Testament, and even related words are uncommon (see especially Rom 3:24-25; Heb 2:17). The sense is "expiation" (of sins), not "propitiation" (of God). The Day of Atonement ritual, with its connection among blood, cleansing, and atonement, stands in the background (see Lev 16, especially vv. 15-16, 30). Given the author's frequent appeals to "the beginning," this language of purification from sin, and that of light and darkness, may be partly intended to recall the readers' experience of baptism (Eph 5:6-11; Col 1:13-14; Heb 10:22-23), just as 1 John ends with language reminiscent of conversion to Christianity from paganism. The author thus seems to be establishing connections with common Christian experience beyond the specifically Johannine tradition, perhaps as a way of strengthening his footing in the conflict with the opponents.

The term translated "advocate" in 2:1 is *parakletos*, which is not used of Jesus elsewhere in the New Testament. In the Gospel of John (but again not elsewhere) it is used of the Holy Spirit (14:16-17, 26; 15:26; 16:7-11). How these two uses are to be related is a difficult question. John 14:16 calls the Spirit *another* advocate, implying that Jesus had already been one, and there is a near identity of function between the Paraclete and Jesus in John 14:15-21. Thus, it may be that this role was already ascribed to Jesus when the Gospel was written. The Spirit is an advocate toward the world rather than toward God, however, while *parakletos* here seems to have its common meaning of sponsor or patron, someone who could influence a court or a powerful person in one's favor (Grayston 1981, 70-80). The notion of an advocate in heaven who intercedes for God's people is well attested in the Hebrew Scriptures and ancient Judaism (e.g., Job 16:19-21; 33:23-26; Zech 1:12-13; 2 Macc 15:12-16; Matt 18:10; *1 Enoch* 47:2; 89:76-77; *T. Levi* 3:5-7; 5:6; *3 Apoc. Bar.* 11-16). However, this advocacy is generally for the suffering people or those falsely accused, not for sinners, for whom only earthly advocates intercede (Gen 20:7; Exod 32:11-14, 30-32; 1 Sam 12:19-25; Job 42:8-10; *2 Apoc. Bar.* 85:1-3; *As. Mos.* 11:17). In Rom 8:34 and Heb 7:25, however, Jesus is the heavenly advocate toward God for sinners. The New Testament texts, including 1 John, thus seem to combine the role of advocate for sinners with the figure of the heavenly intercessor.

That Jesus is the atonement not just for the sins of the Johannine Christian community but for those of the whole world is a remarkably inclusive statement for the otherwise often closed and world-rejecting 1 John (see the comments on 2:15-17). It is probably derived from John 1:29, and implies that for the author the possibility of mission to the world is still open, that opportunity remains to bring the "word of life" to those totally outside the Christian community. The double Johannine attitude toward the world, as object of salvation and as hostile to both Savior and saved, appears in 1 John in the sharpest possible contrast.

◊ ◊ ◊ ◊

In a context of doctrinal controversy, we might expect light to be associated with right knowledge or right belief. But in 1 John it is associated with right *behavior*, that is, with love, which is the first issue that the author takes up after the prologue. The subject of Christology does not return until 2:18-27. This suggests that, although scholars tend to think of the christological conflict as being the root of the problems about mutual love, in the author's mind this priority did not exist. Rather, Christology and ethics are deeply intertwined: it is in Jesus that God is revealed as light and as love, and this revelation includes the commandment to love one another.

This intertwining extends to John's theology proper. At first glance, the two definitions of the "message," in 1:5 and 3:11, seem quite different: the one here is theological, the one there is ethical. However, 1:5–2:11 taken as a whole shows that the aim of the theological statement is also ethical. "God is light" is not so much a statement about God's nature in itself as a metaphor for the loving character of God's relations with humanity (Bultmann 1973, 16). God's action for humanity in Jesus is wholly characterized by love, and human action illuminated by God cannot be any different. For 1 John, none of the theological and soteriological issues that grow out of the Johannine tradition can be separated from love for one another. In this sense, 1 John's theology is fundamentally ethical.

For this very reason, the author's one-sided use of the metaphor of light must be interpreted carefully. This metaphor has often been distorted in the context of unjust relationships between light and dark *peoples*. First John 1:5 is a metaphor that makes an ethical, more than an ontological, statement about God, a statement made more directly in 4:8. Any interpretation of the metaphor that leads away from love, by absolutizing light as good and darkness as bad, would represent a misunderstanding of it.

The overall theme of 1:5–2:2 is integrity and self-deception. First John is committed to a kind of ethical realism, to opposing the denial of reality, whether the reality of our own nature or that of Jesus. On the one hand, to claim sinlessness flies in the face of the realities of human nature. On the other hand, as later passages will assert, the transformation brought about by relationship with God through Jesus Christ must not remain a matter of spiritual fantasy, but is meant to become concrete reality in the ethical character of daily life. Those who claim to be without sin lack both the truth and God's word. In the Johannine writings, "truth" means not simply human honesty, but reality, the reality of God. Denying that we are sinful makes even God untrue, and not just because God has said (in some unspecified place) that people are sinful. Rather, denying our sinful nature means losing the knowledge of God's nature as well, including God's nature as "faithful and just to forgive." Part of the truth missing in those who claim sinlessness is that God is love (4:8, 16). Only by trusting in God's loving faithfulness and justice can we be cleansed of our injustice; it cannot come by making hollow, self-deifying claims to be without injustice already. This strong sense of differentiation between the divine nature and human nature seems fundamental to 1 John. Paradoxically, for human beings to share in the divine nature, the divine truth, they must first admit their own human nature, the human sin. Yet they can do this in full confidence that it is God's nature to love and to forgive, and that this divine love is incarnate in the human Jesus, the Son of God.

## WALKING IN THE LIGHT AND KEEPING THE COMMANDMENTS (2:3-11)

This is the second part of the larger section 1:5–2:11. It is marked off from the first part by a transitional *kai* ("now"), and by the use of a new but equally careful structure. There are three "boasts" or claims in the section, each introduced by "whoever says" (vv. 4, 6, 9), and each preceded by a preparatory statement. Verse 3, with its references to "knowing him" and to keeping the commandments, prepares for the first claim in verse 4; the last part of verse 5, which speaks of being "in him," prepares for the second claim in verse 6; and verse 8 ends with a reference to light, which is then taken up as the third claim in verse 9.

Within this structure, each claim stands at the head of a small unit (vv. 4-5, 6-8, 9-11), while the preparatory statements in verses 5b and 8b are also integral parts of the first two boast units. There is thus an even more careful "chaining" from boast to boast than in 1:5–2:2. This is partially obscured in many translations, including the NRSV, by punctuating with a period before verse 5b ("by this we may be sure that we are in him") and with a lesser break after it. This punctuation recognizes the preparatory function of the statement, but not its place within the first boast unit. Verse 5b not only sets up verse 6 but also rounds off verses 4-5, and indeed reaches back to the language of verse 3. Thus, we should probably place a period at the end of verse 5, and see "by this" as meaning "by obeying his word" rather than as referring forward to verse 6.

As in 1:5–2:2, the symmetry is not perfect. The first and third boasts (vv. 4-5, 9-11) both have a claim, an improper action that contradicts the claim, a resulting status, and a contrasting statement about those who take the proper action, stating or implying that they fulfill the claim. The second boast (v. 6) is quite different in form, essentially combining the claim (to "abide in him") and the proper action ("ought to walk just as he walked"). Also as in 1:5–2:2, there is no obvious logical progression from one boast unit to the next. Indeed, one might regard all of the claims, and all of the proper actions, as essentially equivalent in Johannine thought.

◊ ◊ ◊ ◊

For sentences that seem so straightforward, in Greek as in English, the statements in this section contain a surprising number of the grammatical and semantic ambiguities that can make 1 John so baffling. For instance, to whom do the pronouns "he/his/him" in verses 3-6 refer? Following 2:2, the most obvious answer is Jesus, so that the subject of the unit would be knowing Jesus and keeping his commandments. However, since verse 3 begins a new section, its pronouns do not necessarily carry over from verse 2. Elsewhere in these epistles (in contrast to the Gospel of John) it is generally *God* rather than Jesus who gives commandments (1 John 3:22-24; 4:21; 5:2-3; 2 John 4-6). The language of "knowing" and of "being in" or "abiding in" is also applied to God slightly more often than to Jesus. (On these issues, see the introduction.) Despite the difficult break with verse 2, then, "he" probably refers to God in verses 3-6*a*. On the other hand, "to walk just as he walked" in verse 6*b* must surely refer to Jesus and not God. This is signaled not only by the sense but by the use of a different pronoun for "he" (*ekeinos* rather than *autos*), one that elsewhere in 1 John is only used in speaking about the imitation of Jesus (3:3, 5, 7, 16; 4:17). Thus introduced, Jesus is apparently referred to again in verse 8, this time with *autos*. We must therefore probably distinguish a reference to God in verses 3-6*a* from a reference to Jesus in verses 6*b*, 8 (so REB, CEV), although it remains just possible that all the pronouns refer to Jesus. Many of the statements probably represent traditional formulas that the readers would have understood despite this ambiguity.

"In this we know that" (NRSV: "by this we may be sure that") in verses 3 and 5 is the first of the discernment formulas that are common throughout 1 John. The type found here, which tells how to confirm that something is true, also appears in 3:19, 24; 4:13; 5:2; there is a somewhat similar one in 2:18 (see also 2:29; 3:14). Two other types also occur: "to know [someone or something] in (or from) this" (3:16; 4:2, 6); and "in this" accompanied by an explanatory statement (3:10; 4:9, 10, 17). In every case, the criterion for the discernment is an action taken by people or by God (see also 3:6; 4:20-21).

These formulas present ways of recognizing a number of things very important to the author: being God's children, being of the truth, the Spirit of God, love. First John is deeply concerned with distinguishing the real from the false in such matters. The claims laid out in this section—knowing God, abiding in God, being in the light—would have been made by both the author and his opponents. The point of the section is to articulate criteria—keeping

God's word or commandments, walking as Jesus walked, loving one's brothers and sisters—for testing the validity of such claims, and thus implicitly to show that the opponents' claims are invalid. The similarity to the other discernment formulas noted above may suggest that the author makes no sharp distinctions among the criteria, or among knowing, loving, and abiding in God. All are aspects of the one concern that dominates 1 John, enabling the readers to discern what and who truly belongs to the realm of God and eternal life.

The subject of knowing God is introduced rather suddenly here. It was a major religious ideal in ancient culture, by no means restricted to Gnosticism. "Knowing God," in biblical language, does not mean knowing correct facts or doctrines about God, but having an intimate relationship with God. The prophets of the Hebrew Scriptures associated the people's failure to know God with sin, and promised that God would one day grant them full knowledge (Jer 9:6, 23-24; 31:34; Hos 4:1; 6:1-3; Hab 2:14). Though the Johannine writings do not speak of the new covenant promise, its fulfillment may be in the background of their stress on the knowledge of God given through Jesus (Malatesta 1978; see further below on "abiding"). In 1 John, the question of knowing God is part of the conflict with the opponents. In the Johannine tradition, knowledge of the true God is demonstrated by fidelity to Jesus (e.g., John 8:19, 54-55; 14:7; 15:21-24; 17:3, 25-26), who revealed God as love in his own sacrificial death (1 John 4:8-10, 14-16; 5:20). By proposing criteria that undercut the opponents' claim to know God, the author recalls the rebukes and promises of the prophets and also puts the opponents on the wrong side of the Johannine dualism. In this way, he not only shows the readers what they must do and assures them of their position when they do so, but also pulls them toward his own side in the conflict.

The parallel between keeping the commandments and keeping the word in verses 4-5, and the explicit identification of commandment and word in verse 7, strongly suggest that the two are synonymous in 1 John, although there may be times when they are distinguished in the Gospel of John. On the other hand, there may be a development from keeping the commandments in general in

verses 3-5 to keeping the specific commandment of love in verses
7-11 (on all this, cf. von Wahlde 1990, 21-30, 55-60). The ideas
here have deep roots in Johannine tradition (John 14:15, 21-24),
and beyond that in Hebrew Scripture. In Deuteronomy, keeping
God's commandments or word often simply means obeying God,
without reference to specific rules (e.g., Deut 4:40; 8:6; 13:4; 29:9).
But it is not the law of Moses as a whole, or even the Ten
Commandments, that 1 John has in mind. Later on, the author will
speak of two commandments, believing rightly in Jesus and loving
one another (3:23). In this first instance, however, he names only
the commandment of love as *the* commandment. The proof of
knowing God is keeping God's commandments, and the commandment in question is love.

Having the love of God made perfect and being in God (v. 5), in
their relation to loving one another (vv. 6-11), anticipate the
discussion in 4:11-18. However, it is not certain that "the love of
God" here means God's love for us (subjective genitive) as it does
in 4:12 (and in 3:17; 4:9). It can also mean our love for God
(objective genitive), as in 5:3 (probably also in 2:15). The precise
content of verse 5 is closer to 5:3 than to 4:12, and in the context
here God is also the object of knowing and abiding. The parallel
with John 14:23-24 is significant as well. "Of God" in verse 5 is
therefore probably objective: love *for* God is perfected in those who
keep God's word. (For the meaning of "perfection," see the comments on 4:12.)

The claim to abide in God (v. 6) was evidently shared by the
author and his opponents. This use of the term "abiding" is
virtually unique to the Johannine writings, not only in the New
Testament but in hellenistic religious literature in general. Its one
notable precursor is the new covenant promise that God would
come to dwell among and within the people (Ezek 36:26-27;
37:26-28), who would thus know God (Jer 31:31-34). The Johannine claims, however, go beyond even this (Malatesta 1978). The
verb *menō* implies both inhabiting a place and remaining there over
time. In 2:6, 10 (where the NRSV has "lives"), abiding is not inertia
but *walking* as Jesus walked (Heise 1967, 123). Elsewhere in the
epistles, the aspect of duration comes to the fore, since the author

is concerned that the readers persist in what they have heard "from the beginning" (see 1 John 2:17, 24, 27; 3:9, 14; 2 John 2, 9). In the Gospel of John, Jesus always stands as intermediary between Christians and God (15:7-10; 17:21-23); in 1 John, however, they can abide (or simply "be") directly in God and God in them (2:5-6; 3:24; 4:12-16; they abide in Jesus in 2:27-28; 3:6, and in both in 2:24; 5:20; see further the introduction). Note that though "abiding" certainly implies union with the divine, it plainly excludes a complete identity.

Those who claim to abide in God are obliged to imitate the "walk" of Jesus, perhaps partly because in the Gospel of John it is Jesus who is in God (John 10:38; 14:10-11, 20; 17:21-23). Imitation of Jesus is a major ethical category in 1 John. As frequently elsewhere, it is signaled by the pronoun *ekeinos*, "he" (discussed above), and the verb *opheilō*, "ought" (3:16; 4:11). Imitation of God was introduced in 1:5-7, and imitation of both God and Jesus is a dominant theme in 2:28–3:10 (see the comments there). Here and in 3:16; 4:7-18, its essence is plainly love. In the Gospel of John, Jesus' disciples are also to love one another as he has loved them (13:13-17, 34-35; 15:12-13). Such use of examples for the reader to imitate is naturally common in moral exhortation (see 1 Cor 4:16; Phil 3:17; 1 Thess 2:14; 2 Thess 3:6-13; Poly. *Phil.* 9; and the catalogs in Heb 11:4-38; *1 Clem.* 9-12; 17-18; 55). Imitation of Christ is especially important in such texts (e.g., Rom 15:1-7; Eph 4:32–5:2; Heb 13:11-14; 1 Pet 2:21-25). In these passages, it is Jesus' self-giving that is the object of imitation, and that is the case here also, as the subsequent discussion of the love commandment shows. Imitation of the divine is rooted in the holiness precepts of Lev 11:44-45; 19:2; 20:26; 21:8. In the teaching of Jesus, *mercy* replaced holiness as the focus of imitation (Luke 6:35-36; Matt 18:23-34). This revision, albeit narrowed in scope, is preserved in the Fourth Gospel's commandment that Jesus' disciples imitate his own love, and is continued in 1 John's stress on the imitation of both Jesus and God. First John thus reflects a widespread theme; but the centrality of the theme here and the profundity of its role at the intersection of theology and ethics is rarely matched elsewhere.

The discussion of the commandment in verses 7-8 grows out of the obligation expressed in verse 6. Unfortunately, its grammar and logic are very obscure. Is the "old commandment" the same as the "new commandment," and if so, what is it and how can it be both old and new? What is it that is "true," and how is it true "in him and in you"? How does all this relate to darkness and light?

Commentators generally agree that the old and new commandments are the same. That it is both "old" and "new" most likely has to do with its content. As verses 9-11 will make clear, this commandment is the commandment to love one another (John 13:34-35; 15:12, 17). It is an old commandment, therefore, because the readers are familiar with it from the Gospel of John, or at least from Johannine tradition. It is "the word that [they] have heard," which they have "had from the beginning." In 2:23-24 what the readers have "heard from the beginning" is a christological confession (see also 1:1); but in 3:11, as here, the message heard from the beginning is none other than the commandment to love one another (see the comments there and on 1:5). From their first days as Christians, the readers have known the commandment to imitate Jesus in love.

Then how is this old commandment new? In part, the author is simply playing on words: the love commandment was known to the readers as the "new commandment" (John 13:34). But the commandment is still new for the same reason that it was called new in the Gospel: it is the *eschatological* commandment. The New Testament claim that Jesus is the Messiah is a claim that the eschatological age, the age of God's reign, has begun. Here this claim is expressed using the metaphor of dawn: the new age, ruled by the God who is light (1:5), has already begun to shine, as the darkness of the old fades away (see also John 1:5, 9). Because it is a new age, the commandment of love that characterizes it is also new.

The expression in verse 8 rendered "that is true in him and in you" by the NRSV is problematic. "That is true" is neuter in Greek *(ho estin alēthes)*, and thus does not agree in gender with the feminine "commandment" *(entolē)*. Although many English translations make the *commandment* what is true, this is grammatically impossible. The relative pronoun could refer to the preceding statement as such, so that the *newness* of the commandment would be true (so the KJV; Brooke 1912, 36; Marshall 1978, 129; Strecker 1996, 50). However, it is hard to see the point of insisting on the truth of this newness. More likely, the author wants to stress that the *content* of the commandment is true. The relative clause, then, expresses this content: "Yet I am writing you a new commandment, that which is true in him and in you" (Westcott 1892, 53; Klauck 1991, 120).

Note that the author does not speak of what *was* true in him, but of what *is* so: the truth in Jesus still endures. In Johannine terms, what is "true in him" would be the truth from God, the divine reality, that Jesus brought (see the comments on "doing the truth" in 1:6). Indeed, Jesus himself is this truth (John 14:6). By saying that the new commandment is identical with what was and is "true" in Jesus, 1 John asserts that *the revelation of God in Jesus Christ is not to be distinguished from the commandment of love* (see 4:8-9). It is this truth revealed in Jesus that is not found in those who neglect the commandment (v. 4), and it is this revelation that is pushing back the darkness and letting the true light shine in eschatological newness.

The revelation is also true "in you," for according to the Gospel of John, disciples are to know the truth and to be consecrated in it (John 8:31-32; 17:17). Thus, "that which is true in him and in you" is the word heard long since, the commandment of love revealed by God in Jesus, as valid in the readers as it was and is in him. The eschatological community shows that it is eschatological by its adherence to the messianic new commandment. It is now in the readers that this truth must be demonstrated, and that is why the author is writing: to bring to their mind the old new commandment, lest they be deceived by those who offer some other way to know and abide in God, a novel way that does not involve loving one another, an understanding of the revelation in Jesus that does not include the love commandment.

Verses 9-11 at last identify the commandment that the author has been discussing. They also make an inclusion by returning to the subject of walking in darkness or in light (1:5-7), which are now identified as hating or loving one's brother or sister. Johannine dualism knows no middle ground: failure to love is not simply indifference, but hatred. It is thus hatred that separates one from fellowship with God and prevents one from abiding in God, who is both light and love (1:5; 4:8, 16). The author implies elsewhere that it is the opponents who hate those whom they should love (3:11-17; 4:20-21). In this hatred he may have included their breaking fellowship with the community (2:19), and certainly their failure to care for those in need (3:17). The actions of the opponents must have caused considerable stress and loss of cohesion within the community. One reason for the author's emphasis on mutual love, then, is a desire to restore the community's lost solidarity.

These verses contain the first occurrences in 1 John of the term "brother" *(adelphos),* a masculine form often used generically, hence NRSV "brother or sister" and "another believer" (see the comments on "young people" in 2:12-14, however). Most of its appearances cluster where the topic is mutual love: 2:9-11; 3:10-17; 4:20-21. Despite the universalism often thought to be implied by the term "brotherly love," the reference in 1 John is to other Christians, not to human beings in general. This is clear, for example, in 5:16. The typically Johannine form of the love commandment is "love *one another"* (John 13:34-35; 15:12, 17; 1 John 3:11, 14, 23; 4:7, 11-12; 2 John 5). The author may even be thinking solely of members of the Johannine community (see further below). If the opponents devalued material reality (4:2-3; 5:6-8) and focused on the individual, then mutual love may not have concerned them, even among themselves, much less toward other Christians. Therefore, the author maintains, they do not abide in the divine light, as they claim, but in darkness. They remain in the old age, among the desires of the world that are passing away (2:17), in death rather than the new, eschatological life (3:14).

Love for one another was also characteristic of the Essenes (Josephus *J.W.* 2 §119) and is prominent at Qumran (e.g., 1QS 1:9-11; 7:4-9; 10:17-19; CD 6:20–7:3). It appears throughout the *Testaments of the Twelve Patriarchs* as well (e.g., *T. Iss.* 5:2; *T. Gad* 6:1-3; *T. Jos.* 17:2-3). The Qumran scrolls (but not the *Testaments*) also promote hatred for those outside the sect. This does distinguish them from the Johannine writings; but though 1 John decries hatred of sisters and brothers, Johannine love, limited to the community, by no means precludes hostility to the outside world (see the comments on 2:15-17).

Verses 10-11 vividly exploit "walking" as a metaphor for one's way of life. The language of stumbling, walking in the dark, and blindness is reminiscent of the claims of the Johannine Jesus (John 8:12; 9:4-5, 39-41; 11:9-10; 12:35-36). By alluding to these claims, the author unites belief in Jesus with love for one another: Those without love have lost "the light of the world" as well. They stumble in a darkness that is not simply an environment but a force, one that blinds them so that they lose their moral bearings and do not know where they are going.

◊ ◊ ◊ ◊

There is an apparent logical difficulty in 2:4 as compared with 1:8, part of the overall problem of sin in 1 John. The author seems to say that, in order to be truthful, one must neither sin (2:4) nor deny that one sins (1:8). Yet both statements are obviously true: no one can honestly claim either never to sin, or to know God while ignoring God's will. As noted in the concluding comments on 1:5–2:2, access to truth, to the reality of God, is only possible for those who acknowledge the ungodliness in their own human nature. Here the author adds that they must also immerse themselves in the ways of God. Those who desire to know God, to have the truth, must both acknowledge their distance from God and embrace that which comes from God. Much as we might wish it, however, the author does not speak of process or growth here, of moving from sinfulness toward faithfulness. Instead, we simply seem to have a paradox: people of the truth keep God's commandments, and yet also acknowledge their sin that requires God's forgiveness. (See further the comments on 1:7-10; 3:6, 9.)

By the end of this section, we have come full circle to where we began in 1:5. Any claim to relationship with God, who is light, must be tested for its coherence with the light. Though correct teaching about Christ will claim much of the author's attention in 1 John, the test here is not doctrinal purity. Nor is it institutional loyalty, intellectual understanding, or even moral perfection. Rather, the criterion is love, here as elsewhere in the Johannine literature the one significant ethical category. Though commentators often speak of 1 John's opponents as morally lax, the author never introduces any detailed moral code. The test is only and simply to love; but the seeming ease and naiveté of this test are lessened when we observe in 3:16-17 what 1 John means by love.

A disturbing yet inescapable part of 1 John's Johannine heritage is its restriction of this love to "brothers and sisters" within the Christian community. Such a perspective is not uncommon in sociologically sectarian groups, and the Johannine call to love one another is not without enduring value (see the introduction). Of course, we know little about how well the Johannine Christians succeeded in carrying out this commandment; the epistles are not actually very encouraging in this regard. Nevertheless, the Johannine "new commandment" continues to stand as a peculiar challenge, an ideal way of life in itself, yet only a part of the love of neighbor and even of enemies proclaimed by Jesus.

For the Johannine writers, the love commandment is new because its revelation in Jesus already began the new, eschatological age. The Gospel of John had given a powerful presentation of early Christian "realized" eschatology, the conviction that eschatological things are already becoming real, that the messianic age is present in what is happening because of Jesus. First John is sometimes thought to represent a decline from this faith, the love commandment having become something old, a matter of tradition (Conzelmann 1954, 198-99). In its vision of the new commandment thrusting back the night of hatred, however, 1 John still maintains a vividly realized eschatology. The readers have known this commandment throughout their lives in the Johannine community; yet it remains a sign of the eschatological nature, the radical newness of that community that they imitate Jesus by loving one another.

It is true that for 1 John the Christian community allows the light to continue shining by continuing to proclaim the message inaugurated by Jesus (Klein 1971, 289-91). This continuation, however, is not only a matter of message but of action, of walking as Jesus walked; or rather, the message and the action are one. Imitation of the suffering and the self-giving love of Christ is one of the wellsprings of Christian ethics in the New Testament, and has continued so throughout Christian history. "Imitation" in this sense means neither mimicry of Jesus' lifestyle nor attempting to become like him through moral endeavor (Yoder 1972, 133-34; Webster 1986). Rather, those who claim to be enlightened, to know God, can verify that claim only by their concrete correspondence to the one who brought this knowledge into the world, and to the nature of the God that he revealed as love. This kind of imitation, then, also continues to proclaim his revelation.

The imitation of Jesus had a special importance in our author's situation, because it implied an affirmation of the saving value of Jesus' life and death that the opponents would probably have denied. This interweaving of ethical and christological motifs is a constant feature of 1 John. It reminds us that, in spite of the Protestant insistence on faith as prior to works and the intellectual distinction between theology and ethics, at the bedrock level of Christianity the two are experienced as one thing. Believing and loving are two aspects of a single human response to divine love, so that Christians can exercise neither one authentically without the other (Feuillet 1972, 326-27). It is precisely this unity that 1 John defends throughout.

## CONQUERING THE WORLD (2:12-17)

There are two short sections here, 2:12-14 and 2:15-17, each formally self-contained and related to the other only by the theme of opposition to the world and the evil one. The themes of forgiveness of sins and knowing God are continued from 1:5–2:11, but the lack of any obvious connection to 2:18-27 typifies the structural obscurity that makes 1 John so difficult to interpret. At least verses 12-14, however, do represent a type of digression known in ancient rhetoric (Watson 1989a). The effect may thus have been more impressive for the first readers than for modern ones.

The most tightly structured unit in 1 John, 2:12-14 consists of two highly symmetrical sets of three statements about the author's reasons for writing (cf. the two sets of three boasts in 1:5–2:11). All six statements begin with a form of the verb "write," followed by "to you (plural)" and the name of a group, then the conjunction *hoti* ("because" or "that") and an assertion about the group. The first three (vv. 12-13) use the present tense, "I am writing." The second three (v. 14) have the aorist, a past tense that can be used in epistolary contexts to refer to the letter in hand (NRSV "I write"; cf. 2:21). The repetition and variation between the first and second sets of statements, including the change in tense, partly reflect ancient rhetorical practices meant to amplify, enliven, and refine the thought (Watson 1989a, 102-5).

Two different words for "children" are used, *teknia* in verse 12 (as in 2:1 and most other places in 1 John) and *paidia* in verse 14 (also used in 2:18). The two words seem synonymous, and are used throughout 1 John to address the readers. Thus, each set of three statements begins by speaking to the *whole* readership, not a group within it. These two general addresses can be seen in relation to the other statements in two ways simultaneously. As will be seen below, each is elaborated by the two statements that follow it. However, the first address to "children" also seems related to what is said in *both* of the addresses to "young people" (since the evil one is related to sinning), while the second address to "children" relates to *both* addresses to the "fathers." The two basic themes, overcoming sin and the evil one and knowing God and Jesus, are thus closely intertwined, and both are associated with 1 John's entire readership.

The following section, 2:15-17, is much more loosely structured. It consists of an admonition against loving the world and three reasons for this admonition. All the reasons center on the contrast between the world and God: one cannot love both; worldly things (three are specified) have an origin that is not God; and the world is fading away while obedience to God is eternal.

◊ ◊ ◊ ◊

If "children" refers to all the readers, then what about "fathers" and "young people"? They could be different groups within the readership, whether the reference to age is literal or metaphorical.

Acquaintance with one who was "from the beginning" seems naturally characteristic of fathers, and conquering strength of young people. However, both the structure of verses 12-14 and usage elsewhere in 1 John (1:10; 2:3-5; 4:6, 7; 5:4-5, 20) suggest that all the traits here are characteristic of *all* believers. "Fathers" and "young people," then, probably do not represent different segments of the community, but reflect a common biblical rhetorical figure used to refer to an entire group (e.g., Exod 10:9; Josh 6:21; Jer 31:13; Ezek 9:6). It should be noted that while the Greek words translated "children" and "little children" include both female and male, the other terms are strictly "young *men*" and "fathers." It is possible that the author intends to include women (Thompson 1992, 29, 63). However, it may also be that women in the community are already losing the prominence that is apparent in the Gospel of John (see John 4:4-42; 11:20-27; 20:11-18; and Perkins 1984, x-xi).

The conjunction *hoti* that introduces each statement about the readers can have various meanings. It could be declarative, introducing the content of the writing: "I am writing to you, little children, *that* your sins are forgiven." But why would the author need to inform people who know the Father, for instance, *that* they know the Father? Rather, *hoti* is probably causal, expressing the author's reasons for writing (1:4; 2:1; 5:13 speak of his purpose). These verses serve the same typically parenetic aim as 2:21, 27, assuring the readers that the author, in writing to them in this way, does not think them ignorant or feeble, but is writing in order to build on the spiritual strengths that they have (cf. 1 Thess 4:1, 9-10; 5:1-2). Indeed, some of the assurances suggest that they have passed the tests set out in 1:9-10; 2:3-4. The author, here as elsewhere, is subtly drawing the readers to his side in the conflict by suggesting that they are already in agreement.

It is also typical of parenesis that these assertions about the readers seem to be fixed, well-known formulations or slogans (note how abruptly "his name," i.e., Jesus', is introduced in v. 12), whether they originate in the context of baptism or elsewhere. Only "you are strong" has no parallels. This may be why many of them use the perfect tense, which in Greek refers to past events whose effects continue. The benefits gained on becoming a Christian, which are themselves grounded in the prior victory of Jesus, are displayed in the readers' current status. This assurance then provides a basis for the exhortations that follow.

The connection of forgiveness of sins with Jesus' name (v. 12) is a specialty of Luke–Acts within the New Testament (Luke 24:47; Acts 2:38; 10:43; 22:16), perhaps, like 1 John, drawing on early Christian baptismal traditions. Elsewhere in the Johannine writings, forgiveness of sins is found only in John 20:23 and 1 John 1:9 (see the comments there). The *name* of Jesus, however, is important in the Fourth Gospel, especially in relation to belief (John 1:12; 2:23; 3:18; 20:31). In keeping with ancient concepts, the "name" refers to Jesus' identity as such, his entire being. Belief in this being is part of the christological conflict in 1 John (3:23; 5:13), and so here it is the readers' faith in Jesus, both divine and human, that brings them forgiveness.

"The evil one" as a name for the devil (v. 13), though found elsewhere in the New Testament (including John 17:15), is common only in 1 John (see also 3:12; 5:18-19) and Matthew (5:37; 6:13; 13:19, 38); nor is it known in earlier Judaism. "You have conquered" is quite Johannine, however (despite the NRSV, the same word is used in vv. 13 and 14). Elsewhere it refers to conquering the world (1 John 4:4; 5:4-5; John 16:33), which is in the power of the evil one (1 John 5:19; cf. John 12:31; 14:30; 16:11). "You have conquered the evil one" thus implies that the basis of the readers' eschatological confidence is Jesus, the conqueror of the world, in whose name they believe.

"Him who is from the beginning" (a person, in contrast to 1:1; 2:7, 24; 3:11) must surely mean Jesus, whether "the beginning" means the beginning of Christian tradition or of creation. (The contrast with the evil one and the use of "from the beginning" in 3:8 may suggest that the latter is primary.) "Knowing the Father" is always a matter of knowing Jesus in the Gospel of John (8:19; 14:6-10; 15:21-25; 16:3; 17:3), and it is Jesus who reveals God as love (1 John 4:8-10, 14-16; 5:20), hence the parallel expressions in verse 14. "The word of God abides in you" is also typically Johannine (see 1:10; also John 5:38; 8:31; 15:7). For 1 John, the proof of knowing God is keeping the commandment of love (2:3-4; 4:7-8), which is part of the word of God that abides in the young people.

Thus, each of the two addresses to the readers as "children" is illuminated by the two statements that follow it. In verses 12-13, the readers' sins are forgiven because of the name of the one whom the "fathers" know, and thus the devil, the originator of sin (3:8), is defeated. In verse 14, the readers know God in their knowing Jesus and in their having the divine word in them, the word of love that conquers the evil one. Some of these themes seem related to the new covenant promises of Jer 31:33-34 and Ezek 36:25-27.

The connection in Johannine thought between the evil one and the world provides the continuity, such as it is, between verses 12-14 and verses 15-17. The latter unit turns on a dualistic contrast between the world and God that is noticeably deeper than what is usual in the New Testament, including the Gospel of John. "The world" in Johannine thought sometimes means the whole world created by God and sometimes specifically the *human* world, a system constituted by human choices in opposition to God. First John has both halves of this paradoxical attitude: that God loved the world and desired to save it (1 John 2:2; 4:9, 14; see John 3:16-17; 6:33, 51; 12:46-47), and that the world is the enemy of God, Christ, and Christians (1 John 2:15-17; 3:1, 13; 4:4-5; 5:4-5, 19; in John, see, e.g., 8:23; 15:18-19; 16:8-11, 33; 17:9-16, 25). Yet it lacks the fundamental link between the two halves, namely that the Savior came to the world and was rejected by it (John 1:10-11). The texts in 1 John only make sense if this link is presupposed. Otherwise the world's hostility to God appears to be due to something in its fundamental makeup, and, though 1 John is often thought to be combating Gnostic tendencies, its dualism becomes almost Manichaean.

"The love of the Father" (v. 15) may mean "the Father's love" (subjective genitive) or "love for the Father" (objective genitive); see the comments on 2:5 and 3:17. Other expressions stating what is or is not "in" people favor the former (2:14, for example, as well as 1:8, 10; 2:4; 3:17). However, the parallel with loving the world makes the latter seem slightly more natural. The love in question is *agapē*, the affectionate and self-giving love that ought to be directed to other people and above all to God, not to the fulfillment of self-centered desires.

Only here in the Johannine writings do we read, not of worldly people, but of the *things* that are in the world. Verse 16, however, defines these things as human desire for, and pride in, created objects, not the objects themselves or the pleasure they give. The warning in these verses is against *loving our own desires*. The three genitives are all subjective, not objective, genitives. Thus, "desire of the flesh" is "desire that comes from the flesh," not "desire for the flesh." "Flesh" means self-centered human nature; it is not necessarily a specific reference to sexual desire. In John (1:13, 14; 3:6; 6:63; 8:15), flesh is simply inferior to spirit, as the *merely* human to the divine, not evil in itself. The same is true elsewhere in the epistles (1 John 4:2; 2 John 7). Here, however, it is clearly associated with the world as opposed to God, as is "desire" itself (v. 17). This is in line with other early Christian moral discourse, where aversion to the "desires of the flesh" (e.g., Gal 5:16, 24; Eph 2:3; 1 Pet 2:11; *Did.* 1.4) and "worldly desires" (Titus 2:12; *2 Clem.* 17:3; Poly. *Phil.* 5:3) is a commonplace. This usage is rooted in the language of hellenistic, especially Stoic, moral philosophy (e.g., Epictetus *Diss.* 2.18.8-9), including that of hellenistic Judaism (4 Macc 1:30–2:6; Philo *Spec. Leg.* 1.148-50; 4.92-94). First John, however, focuses on desire as such, not on desires in the plural. What does not come from God, then, is the desire that the flesh, the self-centered self, generates; see also Jas 4:1-4.

"Desire of the eyes" is an unusual phrase, not clearly related to biblical, Jewish, or general hellenistic moral teaching. It may simply mean desire for what can be seen, distinguished from "desire of the flesh" by referring more to the outward stimulation of desire by sensory perception than to its inner source. The "eyes" here may also be the eyes that have been blinded by lack of love (2:11) and therefore give rise to avaricious desire. The Greek word *bios* is etymologically "life" (not the same as *zōē*, used for "eternal life"), but the traditional, vague "pride of life" fails to capture its sense in verse 16. By extension it means "one's means of living, property, wealth," as in 3:17. "Arrogance based on wealth" (REB) or "pride in riches" (NRSV) conveys the intended meaning (see also Wis 5:8, using a different word). Whatever the precise sense of "desire of the flesh" and "desire of the eyes," the author explicitly warns against the attitude that wealth engenders. This attitude separates us from the love of God, because it separates us from the love of others.

This sheds some light on the point of verses 15-17 as a whole. The absence of the love of God within (v. 15) suggests that loving the world is the opposite of loving one's brothers and sisters (3:16-17). The fault thus lies not in created things but in the human responses that make idols of them and deprive us of love. These responses are not extraordinary evils but the normal arrangement of the world, its everyday self-centeredness (Wengst 1978, 97); but precisely as such they are not from God, and are to be rejected. In 1 John's dualism, God and the world are opposed in such a way that things originate in, and are determined by, either the one or the other. Thus it is not possible to love—to give oneself completely to—both at once.

But "the world and its desire are passing away." This is not a reference to their transience in general, but means that they are going the same way as the darkness of hatred (2:8-11). Such things are on the way out as a result of Christ's eschatological conquest of the world and the devil. To do the will of God rather than one's selfish desires means keeping God's commandments, namely, believing in Jesus and loving one another (3:23). Those who do this "abide forever" (AT), because they know God (2:3-4) and so have eternal life (5:11-13, 20; John 17:3). They abide, moreover, not as isolated individuals, but in company with others, whom they love and whose belief they share.

The conflict with the opponents is at most in the background in 2:12-17, but many of the expressions used here were significant in it. Given their Christology, the author would not consider that the opponents know Jesus or God, or that the "name" of Jesus is effective for them. Precisely their refusal to acknowledge any sins to be forgiven would prevent the word of God from abiding in them (1:10). This attitude toward sin may have led them into actions that the author regarded as love for the world; certainly, without love for one another they could not love God (4:20). Elsewhere he places them on the side of the world, which is conquered only by the christological faith that they lack (4:4-5; 5:4-5). Thus, the terms of both the encouragement and the warning here gain added force from the specific situation to which they were addressed.

◊ ◊ ◊ ◊

First John 2:3-8 had spoken of keeping God's commandments, but verses 9-11 specified only one commandment, that of mutual love. The ethical admonitions here are even less precise. That one should not love the world or the things in the world may not mean that one should not enjoy life at all; but it is not hard to see why it has often been interpreted in that way. What is really intended here, however, is comparable to the teaching of Jesus about serving two masters (Matt 6:24). "Instead of worshipping God through His creation we are always trying to worship ourselves by means of creatures" (Merton 1961, 26).

For the dualism of 1 John, sin, the world, and the devil represent real dangers for Christians; yet they have already been substantially overcome by Jesus, and so by those who know him. We see here both the early Christian sense of endangerment in the world and the confidence in God, not fear of God, that our author hoped to evoke. Those who know God, whose lives are conformed to the truth of God, that is, to the word of love revealed in Jesus, gain a share in the eternal life of God, which shines now even as the world passes away. This confidence provides the foundation for the nonworldly (that is, countercultural) lifestyle that is enjoined in 2:15-17.

## THE COMING OF THE ANTICHRIST (2:18-27)

The addresses "children" and "little children" in verses 18 and 28 help to define 2:18-27 as a section, as do the references to anointing in verses 20 and 27. The internal structure of the section consists primarily of units that alternate between speaking about the opponents (vv. 18-19, 22-23a, 26) and the readers (vv. 20-21, 23b-25, 27; note the emphatically placed "you" at the beginnings of vv. 20, 24, and 27). Verse 25, however, seems only loosely attached to its context. Some of the units are connected by means of catchwords (e.g., "lie/liar" in vv. 21, 22).

◊ ◊ ◊ ◊

In this section the christological issue is broached openly for the first time, and the opponents, who were at most hinted at before, are denounced explicitly. The section contains some very obscure syntax, however, and verse 27 in particular requires careful attention. As elsewhere in 1 John, we also find both typically Johannine language (truth, abiding, eternal life) and usages that are more at home elsewhere in early Christianity (antichrist, anointing, promise).

The initial subject here is eschatology, "the last hour" (v. 18). This phrase must be taken in its obvious sense: the end of time is at hand (see Rom 13:11-12; 1 Cor 7:29-31; 1 Pet 4:7). Obviously the author is referring to eschatological teaching well known to the readers, so well known that the appearance of "antichrists" could serve as a definite sign that the last hour has come. There is a similar phenomenon in 1 Tim 4:1-3; 2 Tim 3:1-9. Here, however, the thought is modified through the typical Johannine "realized" eschatology (see the introduction). Eschatological events had already occurred in the coming of Jesus the Messiah (v. 22) and the anointing of believers with the Spirit (vv. 20, 27); the world and its ways were already fading (2:8, 17). That "antichrists" should appear is only one more aspect, though a dramatic one, of this reality.

The term "antichrist" is found only in these epistles in the New Testament (2:18, 22; 4:3; 2 John 7). They consistently associate it with false Christology, but that is plainly their author's innovation. Verse 18 seems to quote an eschatological tradition that had the form "antichrist is coming." This tells us nothing about what the term "antichrist" meant when the readers first heard it, however, except that it signaled the last hour. Thus there are two issues: the origin of the term "antichrist," and our author's transformation of its meaning.

As to the origin, Brown (1982, 333-37) admirably surveys the various figures opposed to God in Jewish and Christian tradition:

the sea monster, the angelic Satan, the evil human ruler, and the false prophet (see also Schnackenburg 1992, 135-39; Brooke 1912, 69-79). Whatever the usages elsewhere in the New Testament, it is really only the false prophet that is relevant to our epistles. The elements in common among Mark 13:5-6, 21-22; 2 Thess 2:3-12, and the Johannine epistles are eschatological lying and deception; and 1 John 4:1-3 speaks explicitly of false prophets. But elsewhere in Judaism and early Christianity, the eschatological captain of evil is generally opposed to *God*. The notion of an anti*christ*, that is, an "anti-*Messiah*," is not found at all in Jewish literature, nor in Christian literature except where it is dependent on 1 and 2 John (e.g., Poly. *Phil.* 7:1). The closest precedent is the idea of the "pseudochrist" or false messiah in Mark 13. Thus, "antichrist is coming" may originally have been a warning against a false messiah.

Because there is nothing like it in the Gospel of John, the idea of the false messiah may have been drawn from non-Johannine Christianity. Any such borrowing must have happened some time earlier, though, since our author expects the readers to know it well. It is also possible that he himself invented the term "antichrist" as a replacement for "pseudochrist." Its sense would be "substitute Christ," but in this context shading into "rival Christ" and then "opponent of Christ." Because of these terminological issues, we should not necessarily read everything said about the eschatological enemy in other Christian texts into the background here. That there are "*many* antichrists" is clearly a new development, aimed specifically at the opponents. First John thus identifies the numerous proponents of a false Christology with the single expected false Christ—a rather bold move. It is the opponents' deceit, in the author's view (1:8; 2:26; 3:7; 4:6; 2 John 7), that justifies the identification. This suggests that the opponents were not merely fellow Johannine Christians who left the group, but *teachers*, people who were in a position to lead, or mislead, others (see further on v. 27).

The wording of verse 19 seems to imply that the opponents initiated some breaking of fellowship with the rest of the Johannine community. They have left the community, but for that very reason they must not really have belonged to—literally, "been of"—it all along, perhaps because they have broken the loving unity that is a mark of Jesus' authentic followers (John 13:34-35; 17:11, 21-23). To "be of" something in Johannine thought means both to originate from it and to belong to it, to share both its essence and its characteristics. To "be of" us is the same as to "be of" Jesus' flock or his disciples (John 10:26; 18:17, 25). Moreover, as used here, "us" includes the readers together with the author, drawing them to share in the sense of betrayal, and binding them to the author against the opponents. Thus, to "be of us" means to belong to the author's party *conceived as identical with the true Johannine community*.

Turning to the readers (v. 20), the author speaks of their "anointing," a somewhat unexpected term. It could refer to anointing as part of the ritual of baptism, although the earliest evidence of such a rite is from the late-second century (Tertullian *Bapt.* 7; perhaps also the Christian Gnostic *Gos. Phil.* 67:27-30; 74:12-21, and the Naassenes in Hippolytus *Ref. Haer.* 5.7.19, 9.21-22). But even if it does refer to a baptismal anointing, it is not the physical rite but the spiritual gift received through it that is in view here. The only other place in the New Testament where Christians are said to be "anointed" is 2 Cor 1:21, in a context that speaks of "sealing" and the Spirit. Luke 4:18 and Acts 10:38 refer to the anointing of Jesus with the Spirit, an idea whose ultimate source is Isa 61:1 (see also 1 Sam 16:13). Verse 27 says that this anointing "abides in you" and "teaches you about all things," similar to what is said about the Spirit in John 14:17, 26. The association of the anointing with truth in verse 27 is also reminiscent of the "Spirit of truth" in John 15:26; 16:13 (see also John 4:23-24; 1 John 4:6; 5:6). Though some see "anointing" as meaning teaching or as being related to God's word (Marshall 1978, 154-55), it remains most likely that it refers to the gift of the Spirit, perhaps as given to Christians at baptism. The author clearly does dispute the opponents' claim that their christological teaching comes from the Spirit (4:1-6). The displacement of "Paraclete" by "anointing" as a term for the Spirit could be connected to the use of Paraclete for Jesus in 2:1: perhaps the author avoids the use of that term for the Holy Spirit because the opponents were using it. It is unclear whether "the Holy One" who gives the anointing means God (who is not so designated anywhere else in the NT, though see Isa 1:4; Hab 3:3; Bar 4:22, 37; Sir 23:9) or Jesus (see John 6:69; Mark 1:24; Acts 3:14; Rev 3:7). Verse 27 may say that the anointing comes from Jesus, though the text is obscure (see the comments there). Elsewhere, however, 1 John thinks of God as the source of the Spirit (3:24; 4:13).

In verse 21 the conjunction *hoti* appears three times, and again we encounter the question of whether it is to be translated "that" (declarative) or "because." As in 2:12-14 (see the comments there), the latter is more probable for the first two occurrences: the author's basic intent is to assure the readers that he does not regard them as ignorant, but as knowing the truth (see John 8:32). A sudden shift to "that" for the third *hoti* (NRSV, REB, CEV) would be clumsy (the verb "know" is not repeated in the Greek), but hardly too clumsy for this author. However, the third *hoti* can also be rendered "because" (NIV, NJB, NAB, NEB): the author writes not only because the readers know the truth, but because *this* truth is incompatible with any lie—namely, with the opponents' Christology, the lie that "Jesus is not the Christ" (see v. 22). (On 1 John's concern with lying and liars, see the comments on 1:6.)

Given the parallel with "the antichrist," the liar in question may be an *eschatological* one (see 2 John 7; 2 Thess 2:9-10). But what exactly does the denial that Jesus is the Christ mean? Most commentators (e.g., Dodd 1946, 55-56; Bultmann 1973, 38; Brown 1982, 352; Schnackenburg 1992, 145-46) believe that it means denying that the human Jesus is the divine Christ, ascribing all spiritual significance to the latter (see also 4:2-3; 5:1, 5-8). This would seem to put the opponents on the way toward such second-century heresies as those of the Docetists or Cerinthus (see the introduction). This seems an awkward way to express such an idea, however, and it has been suggested that the opponents, like the Jewish opponents in the Gospel of John, simply do not accept the messiahship of Jesus (Robinson 1962, 131; Stegemann 1985, 292-93; Smalley 1984, 113-14 allows both possibilities; see also the survey in Beutler 1989, 98-103). One intriguing form of this position is taken by José Porfirio Miranda (1977, 156-71), who sees in the opponents' denial that Jesus is the Messiah a denial of eschatological hopes for a reign of love and justice. The christological denial would thus be directly linked to the lack of love for which 1 John also criticizes the opponents, and which it also connects with lying (1:6; 2:4).

It is hard to imagine Christians in the Johannine tradition saying, "Jesus is not the Messiah" (see John 20:31). The opponents are accused of going forward, not backward (2 John 9). It seems more probable, then, that they severed the identity between "Jesus" and "the Christ" and valued only the latter, in the belief that they were receiving new truth from the Spirit (4:1-3; John 15:13). Because this was an innovation, the author calls on the readers to hold to the original teaching "from the beginning" (v. 24). He may also be deliberately shaping his accusation so as to align the opponents with the earlier Jewish opposition, part of his strategy of associating them with "the world." The language of confession and denial in verses 22-23 is deeply rooted in the history and tradition of the Johannine community (see the comments on 3:23). By presenting the opponents' devaluation of Jesus' humanity as a rejection of the classical Johannine confession of Christ, 1 John can declare it a lie ipso facto.

It is also classically Johannine to say that denial or confession of the Son means denying or having the Father (v. 23; see John 5:23; 8:19; 14:6-11; 15:23-24). "Having the Father" is probably to be explained by the parallel in 1 John 5:12, where "having the Son" means believing in and confessing the true Christology. Thus, "having the Father" means acknowledging God rightly by rightly acknowledging Jesus (see also 2 John 9). However, *relationship* with the Father and the Son is also involved, given the claim—typical for 1 John—that the believer abides in God and vice versa (vv. 24, 27; see the comments on 2:6). The readers can maintain this relationship by keeping what they heard "from the beginning" (v. 24) abiding in them (see John 5:38; 8:31; 15:7), an expression that evokes not only the traditional Christology but also the love commandment (2:7-11; 3:11; note the combination of the two with "abiding" in 3:23-24; 4:15-16).

Verse 25, which seems rather detached from its surroundings, combines the characteristic Johannine theme of eternal life with the notably non-Johannine motif of "promise." The latter is much more a Pauline term (e.g., Rom 4:13-16; 2 Cor 1:20; Gal 3:15-22; also important in Hebrews, e.g., 6:11-18; 11:9-13), and may show the infiltration into 1 John of ideas from other Christian groups. Interestingly, it is primarily the later epistles of the New Testament that make a connection between "promise" and "life" (2 Tim 1:1; Titus 1:2; Jas 1:12). In keeping with the usage elsewhere, the maker of this promise is probably to be understood as God (1 John 5:10-11).

Verse 27, especially its second half, exemplifies the frustratingly obscure syntax so common in 1 John. The NRSV treats verse 27b as one long comparison: "But as his anointing teaches you about all things, and is true and is not a lie, and just as it has taught you, abide in him." Raymond E. Brown (1982, 360-61) suggests dividing it into two separate comparisons: "Rather, inasmuch as his anointing teaches you about all things, it is true and free from any lie; and just as it taught you, so you are to abide in him" (similarly NAB, REB, CEV). This, however, leaves the first comparison without much point; probably there is just a single, if rather awkward, comparison. "Is true and is not a lie" is evidently parenthetical, and "just as" resumes the first "as."

This concluding verse, referring back to verses 20 ("anointed") and 24 ("abide"), ties the section together. As in verse 20, the anointing probably means the Holy Spirit, and the identity of the one who gives it is unclear. "Abide in him" at the end surely means Jesus, who may therefore also be the giver of the Spirit. However, 2:2-3, 28-29 show that a sudden shift of reference from God to Jesus here is also possible (see the comments there). By heeding the anointing of the Spirit, the readers can learn all that they need to know. The anointing will also defend them against deception, since it is true and so will teach them only the truth—namely, that they should abide in Jesus. The change from the present "teaches" to the aorist "taught" may be to remind the readers that this is not only the current teaching but one "from the beginning" (v. 24). In fact, abiding in Jesus is already important in the Gospel of John (6:56; 15:1-10), where it implies not only spiritual communion but holding fast to the confession of Jesus as

Messiah in the face of persecution. Likewise here, the readers are urged to "abide" in the Christology of incarnation against the opponents' novelties.

Having the Spirit, the readers need no human teacher. This egalitarianism is a genuinely Johannine theme (John 14:26; 16:13). It may represent the fulfillment of the new covenant promise that God would teach the people directly (Isa 54:13; Jer 31:33-34; note John 6:45). In this assertion the author gives another reason not to listen to the opponents, and a further assurance of his respect for the readers' competence (v. 21; 2:12-14), continuing his rhetorical quest to win their allegiance. The assertion cuts both ways, however—the opponents have no right to teach (whether they claim to do so or not); but the author also cannot claim to teach the readers (which the opponents may have accused him of doing). Yet the address to the readers as "children," so typical of 1 John, is characteristic of a teaching relationship in the Wisdom tradition (e.g., Prov 5:1; 7:24; 8:32; Sir 6:18, 23, 32); and, as noted above, the opponents' christological utterances could also be considered teaching. Thus, both the author and the opponents are in the difficult position of doing what teachers do in a community that claims to need no teacher but the Spirit, who inspires every member. This tension between the role of authoritative teachers and the freedom of each believer to be taught by God has persisted in various ways throughout Christian history.

By identifying the opponents with the expected antichrist, the author has transferred the concept of a leader of evil *outside* Christianity to the realm of *internal* Christian dissension. This is a step with potentially dangerous consequences, the first of many such identifications in Christian history. It opens the way for Christians who disagree with other Christians to demonize them altogether, as indeed the author will do in chapter 3.

At the end of this section, the author puts forward a powerfully antiauthoritarian, nearly anarchic concept of the church and of Christian doctrine, by declaring that the only teaching needed is that which comes directly from the Spirit. The opponents probably invoked the same Paraclete texts of the Fourth Gospel to make the same point in support of their ideas (see the comments on 4:1-3). By what criterion can such claims and counterclaims be evaluated? The author appeals to what the readers had "heard from the beginning." This tradition, he says, is to abide in them; but the Spirit's anointing abides in them too, and the overall result is that the readers will abide in God and Jesus. Thus, these two potentially competing sources of authority, the Spirit and the tradition, both have the same goal, and "abiding" means both interior communion with the divine and persistence in received teaching. The chris-tological tradition continues, but it remains open to interpretation in the community whose members all possess the Spirit. However, the Spirit will not lead the community away from that Christology, as the opponents seem to think, but will teach them to remain steadfastly in it. The Spirit teaches all things, but in so doing it does not undermine what has been present from the beginning. Indeed, the community probably thought of the Spirit as having inspired the original Johannine Christology and the testimony to it in the tradition (5:6-8).

The author does not propose any official authority for safeguard-ing traditional teaching. It is possible, though, to see a kind of incipient "canon" here, a way of evaluating new phenomena in Christian groups. By appealing to tradition handed down from the past, the author is paving the way for the future development of authoritative Christian scripture. (See further the concluding com-ments on 5:6-12.) Yet he does not appeal to the traditional Chris-tology simply because it is traditional, but because of its substance. It enables one to abide in Christ and in God because it truly represents the identity of Jesus Christ. It is not tradition as such but incarnational Christology that furnishes the canon of truth for 1 John.

## LIVING AS CHILDREN OF GOD (2:28–3:10)

The introductory "and now, little children" and the new topic of Christ's being "revealed," that is, his Second Coming, mark 2:28

as the beginning of a new section. At the end, 3:10 reintroduces the topic of love for one another, which enables the transition to 3:11-17. Near both the beginning and the end there are discussions of those who have been born of God, forming an inclusion; indeed, 2:29b is virtually repeated in negative form in 3:10b.

The large amount of patterned repetition in this section makes a variety of structural analyses possible (e.g., Malatesta 1978, 237-38; Antoniotti 1988, 22-23). I would divide the section into two units, 2:28–3:6 and 3:7-10, each of which begins with "little children." The first of these may be further divided into 2:28–3:3 and 3:4-6, the former dealing with the one who "does righteous-ness" (NRSV: "does right") and the latter with the one who "does sin" (NRSV: "commits sin"). These themes are combined in 3:7-10 in a chiastic or concentric structure. Verses 7-8a speak of the one who "does righteousness" and then the one who "does sin"; verse 8b, in the center, speaks of the purpose for which the Son of God was revealed; and verses 9-10 speak of the one who "does *not* do sin" and then the one who "does *not* do righteousness." The overall effect is to contrast as sharply as possible two groups of people and two kinds of actions.

The exegetical observations below will not always respect these structural divisions, given the amount of overlap between them, and given the other patterning in the section. That other patterning includes a series of statements beginning with a Greek participle, usually preceded by "all" (NRSV: "everyone/all/no one/those who . . . "). Most of these can be arranged in pairs of antitheses (similar to 3:6), sometimes by ignoring intervening material. How-ever, rather than giving structure to the section as a whole, these antitheses are woven into other structuring features. For instance, the two pairs in 3:7b//3:8a and 3:9a//3:10b form the chiasm of 3:7-10. Note also that revelation is mentioned with regard to the future and the past in 2:28–3:6, and to the past and the present in 3:7-10; and that the concept of "abiding" appears once in each of the three units (2:28; 3:6, 9).

◊ ◊ ◊ ◊

There are several interrelated themes that run throughout this section: the children of God, likeness to Jesus and to God, righteousness and sin, and revelation. It is notable that in both 2:29 and 3:9-10 the children of God are recognized by their "doing righteousness" and their not "doing sin." Thus, a major aim in the passage is to lay out definitive criteria for identifying God's children, those who are born of God. Elsewhere, 1 John connects birth from God with christological faith (5:1, 4). This connection has deep roots in Johannine theology (John 1:12-13; 3:3-8), though the Fourth Gospel does not fully work out the concept. First John, likewise, is far more concerned with the results of divine birth than with its mechanics. Presumably it is the believers' reception of life from God (5:11) that makes them God's children. A connection of this moment with conversion and with baptism (John 3:5; see also Titus 3:5; 1 Pet 1:3, 23) is at least plausible.

The theme of likeness or imitation appears throughout this section. In 2:28–3:3, it is related to doing what is right, being unknown to the world, seeing and being like God, and purification. In 3:5-6, 7, it is related to sin and righteousness; it is also implicit in the elaboration of this theme in 3:8-10. Righteous actions are not generated by human virtue, nor are they the way to *become* a child of God. They are part of the likeness to God and to Christ (God's preeminent Son) given in a Christian's birth from God. Yet this likeness is not just family resemblance, inherited by the children without any volition on their part. It also results from deliberate imitation (3:3, 7). (On this fundamental ethical theme in 1 John, see the concluding comments on this section and on 2:3-11, and the comments on 2:6.)

Attention to other contexts in 1 John (2:3-11; 3:11-17; 4:7-18) will help us to grasp what is meant by righteousness and sin here. The exhortations to imitate Christ's righteousness (or justice), and even more so his purity, seem reminiscent of the Holiness Code in Leviticus (also discussed in the comments on 2:6). But 2:29; 3:9 base the ability to "do righteousness" rather than sin on birth from God (see also 5:18); and in 4:7 it is those who *love* who are born from God. It is not surprising, then, that 3:10 identifies "doing righteousness" with love. The entire discussion of sin and righteousness in 1 John is thus brought under the heading of love. This is the righteousness and the purity of Jesus that are to be imitated (see 2:6-11; 3:16-18). To "do what is right" does not mean general moral uprightness or adherence to established values, but specifically a love for one another that is carried out in self-sacrifice.

The subject of revelation has already come up in 1 John 1:2. Here it occurs repeatedly, in connection with events of the past, present, and future. Christians look forward to Jesus' revelation, namely, his Second Coming, when their own ultimate divine reality will also be revealed (2:28; 3:2). They look back to his revelation in the incarnation, when he undid sin and the devil (3:5, 8). But there is also a revelation in the present time: The children of God and of the devil are revealed by their doing or not doing righteousness, that is, by their likeness to their "parents" (3:10). "Revelation" thus ties together all the structural units and themes of the section. It also ties together the past, present, and future of Jesus and of the Christian readers. All these revelations are disclosures of reality to the world, the reality of God's Son and God's children. Incarnation and Second Coming are brought into parallel as revelations of Christ; and as there is a continuity between them, so there is a continuity between what believers are and what they will be.

Despite the general thematic clarity of the section, the familiar muddle about pronouns persists (see the comments on 2:3-6). In 2:28 it is probably Jesus whose revelation and coming are anticipated, not God; and in 3:3-7 the pronoun *ekeinos* signals that it is Jesus whose purity and righteousness are to be imitated. Since seeing and resembling Jesus is thus a *present* reality, it may well be God whom believers will one day see and resemble in 3:2 (see further below). At any rate, 2:29b–3:2a clearly speaks of being born of God. We must therefore conclude that the referent of the pronoun "he" *(autos)* shifts abruptly at some point between 2:28 and 3:1. The question is whether it seems harsher to locate the shift at the beginning of 2:29 or in its middle. Does "he is righteous" (2:29a) refer to God (as in 1:9); or does it still refer to Jesus (as in 2:1; 3:7)? Taking the verse in isolation, the natural subject would be God (see, e.g., Deut 32:4; Ps 119:137; Zeph 3:5). Yet the similarity to 3:7 suggests that Jesus remains in view in 2:29a, and that the shift to God takes place after that. As elsewhere, these ambiguities partly result from the author's stringing together of traditional formulas.

"Revealed" in 3:2b has no explicit pronoun for its subject, an unspecified subject being implicit in the Greek verb. Most English versions supply "he"; but it would be grammatically hard to reintroduce Jesus as the subject here, nor is the subject likely to be God. Rather, since "what we will be" was the subject of "revealed" in verse 2a, it probably remains so in verse 2b. We might translate, "Beloved, we are God's children now; and what we will be has not yet been revealed. We do know that when it is revealed, we will be like him [i.e., God], for we will see him as he is."

In the expressions translated "when it is revealed" in 3:2 and "when he is revealed" in 2:28, the conjunction ean, rendered "when," normally means "if." (See John 12:32 for another example of this usage.) Some commentators prefer to take ean in its normal sense (Grayston 1984, 95-97), which would considerably change our understanding of this passage. This is improbable, however, since there are no parallel instances of early Christian writers uncertain if eschatological events will happen. Yet for that very reason, it remains puzzling why our author chooses to use this conjunction.

Though the eschatological terminology in 2:28; 3:2-3 is not found in the Gospel of John, it is used elsewhere in the New Testament: "revealed" (Col 3:4; 1 Pet 5:4); "coming" (parousia, e.g., Matt 24:3, 27, 37, 39; 1 Thess 3:13; 5:23); "hope" (e.g., Rom 8:19-25; 15:4; 1 Thess 4:13; 5:8; Titus 1:2; 2:13; 3:7). The eschatological usage of "confidence" (parrēsia) in 2:28 and 4:17 is unique in the New Testament, however. Placing the traditional Johannine language of abiding in Jesus in this non-Johannine context of future eschatology modifies its thrust. It still means remaining in the Johannine christological confession (see the comments on 2:27), but now also implies continuing in ethical likeness to Jesus (2:29; 3:6), a likeness that gives substance to eschatological confidence.

The Fourth Gospel, with its realized eschatology, does not speak of a future state for believers that will be higher than their present one as God's children (Dodd 1937, 142-43). First John 3:2 is thus closer to non-Johannine forms of early Christian eschatology on this point as well (Matt 5:8; Luke 20:36; 1 Cor 13:12; 15:51-53; Phil 3:20-21; Rev 22:3-4), though the idea of *resembling* the God whom one sees is more at home elsewhere (*Corp. Herm.* 1.26; but note Ps 11:7; 17:15). If the opponents claimed to see God or Christ *now,* or to be like Christ because they had the Spirit (Grayston 1984, 18-19, 101-4; von Wahlde 1990, 145-52), then for them what we will be had indeed already appeared. The author, however, implies that their vision is not a true one, and that that is why they themselves are not like Jesus, why they do not "purify themselves" of sin (3:3-7), that is, do not love their sisters and brothers. It may be that the opponents had an understanding of Johannine tradition that was technically closer to the original realized eschatology on this point. Yet without a desire to be like Jesus in self-giving love, 1 John claims, they have failed to grasp the true meaning of the tradition.

Though it is not gracefully put, the declaration at the beginning of 3:1 forcefully expresses the fundamental Johannine premise from which the ethical conclusions of this section are drawn: Christians are God's children now, and this is the result of God's love given to them (see 4:9-10, 16). It is a commonplace in the Gospel of John that the world that failed to know God also failed to know the one who came from God (John 7:28-29; 8:19, 54-55). In the Gospel, that one is Jesus, and he mediates his unknownness to his disciples (15:18–16:3). Here, however, the Christians' own relation to God causes the world not to know them. The world, focused on itself and its desires (2:15-17), cannot know God or the children of God (contrast 4:5). This self-understanding is typical of sectarian and countercultural groups. It has obvious risks when carried to extremes; but it is also part of what enabled the early Christians, struggling against traditional and widely held social values, to persevere.

"Purity" (3:3) was originally a concept related to the holiness of gods and to ritual and religious practices (see John 11:55; Acts 21:24, 26; 24:18), but came to have a moral reference as well, among both Jews and Gentiles. In the latter sense it is common in the New Testament epistles (Phil 4:8; 1 Tim 4:12; 1 Pet 1:22; 3:2).

Purity was necessary to enter the divine presence (Exod 19:10-11; Ps 24:3-4; Matt 5:8; Jas 4:8), which is also the implication of 1 John 3:2-3. However, "pure" *(hagnos)* and its cognates are never applied to Jesus or to God anywhere else in the New Testament, nor are they ascribed directly to God in the LXX. The only other place in the earliest Christian writings where Jesus is called "pure" seems to be *Herm. Sim.* 5.6.5-6. Evidently our author applied the common religious concept of purity to Jesus in order to sustain his favorite ethical motif: if Christians are to be pure, and so to see God, it must be in imitation of Jesus' purity. The author thus creates an exhortation to moral purity with a christological basis that is unique in early Christianity.

"Lawlessness" or "iniquity" *(anomia)* in 3:4 may refer to the *eschatological* iniquity expected before the last judgment. Second Thessalonians 2:3-12 supplies the strongest support for this (see also Matt 24:11-12; *Did.* 16:3-4). The "lawless one" there may be related to the antichrist of 1 John 2:18-27; 4:1-6, which our author identifies with the opponents. Even without an overtly eschatological reference, the sense would be that sinning shows who is on the wrong side of the dualism defined by the distinction between children of God and of the devil. First John 3:8 makes a clear allusion to John 8:44 (taken up again in 3:15), which the author understands as saying that sinners are offspring of the devil (though, despite NRSV, the word "child" does not appear in the Greek of 3:8). Yet he does not say that they were "born" of the devil, much less when or how such a birth might have happened. First John has no interest in a Gnostic-style myth detailing the origins of those who are saved and those who are not. Its concern is rather to delineate two groups, God's children and the devil's, on the basis of interlocking criteria of belief and action.

The antithetical form of 3:6 establishes two mutually exclusive categories, those who abide in Jesus and those who sin, an unlikeness in contrast to the theme of likeness in 2:28–3:3. (Comparing 3:6 with 2:3-11; 4:8, 16 suggests that the main sin with which the author is concerned continues to be failure to love.) This categorization begins the difficult discussion of sinlessness that 3:7-10 will take up. How can the author say that "no one who abides in him sins," having already rejected the claim that "we have no sin" (1:8, 10; see the comments there)? First John 3:5 sets out two warrants for the assertion of sinlessness: Christ came to take away sins (i.e., acts of sin) and was without sin (as a general quality or principle) himself. "You know" probably indicates that the two warrants are drawn from Johannine tradition. The former is actually stated in John 1:29; the latter could perhaps be inferred from John 7:18; 8:46, and the whole discussion of sin in John 9 (see also Heb 4:15; 7:26). The opponents would no doubt have agreed with both of these warrants; but they may also have claimed that Christ's removal of sins, and even his sinlessness, had been fulfilled in them, that is, that they now "had no sin." The dispute thus concerned the meaning of Johannine tradition: Did it mean that Christ had made believers automatically sinless, whatever their actions might be; or did it mean that they must pattern their actions after Jesus' sinlessness? In other words, is sinlessness a matter of principle or of practice? The author's interpretation would favor the latter, and would also include the means by which Jesus took away sins, namely his death (1:7; 2:2; 4:10), which the opponents apparently considered to be without theological significance (5:6-8).

The assertion of sinlessness in 3:9 raises serious difficulties. One is what the statement that "his *sperma* abides in him" means. The obvious sense is that those who have been born of God possess in themselves a divine element or principle that shields them against any possibility of committing sin. The use of *sperma* for the divine element in human beings, though not in relation to sin, is found in Philo (*Vita Mos.* 1.279) and among Gnostics (*Gos. Truth* 43:3-23; *Ref. Haer.* 7.21.1-22.6; *Adv. Haer.* 1.5.6, 7.2-3, 15.3; *Exc. Theod.* 38.3; 49.1; 53.2; 54.3). The question is how exactly our author understands this element (see the fuller discussions in Brown 1982, 408-11; and Smalley 1984, 172-74). *Sperma* means "seed" or "sperm." Considering 1:10; 2:14, 24 (also John 5:38; 8:31, 37; 15:7), the abiding *sperma* could be the *logos,* the word of God (cf. Jas 1:18; 1 Pet 1:23). Most likely, however, the *sperma,* like the anointing in 2:20, 27, is the Spirit, which is the agent of divine birth (John 3:5-8) and is connected with divine abiding (John 14:16-17; 1 John 3:24; 4:13). It is of course possible that the author would not distinguish between these two, or meant to combine them. There may also be a reference to the covenant promise of God's law and Spirit being implanted in the people to enable their faithfulness (Jer 31:31-34; Ezek 11:19-20; 36:26-27).

Sinlessness thus seems to be, not an ideal to be attained or a potential to be realized, but the inevitable working out of an implanted principle, something that Christians have apart from, or in spite of, their own wills. This extreme form of the idea seems remote from our author's thinking elsewhere; but this only raises the major difficulty of both 3:9 and 3:6, the consistency of their assertions of sinlessness with other statements in 1 John.

There is, of course, exact agreement between 3:6, 9 and 5:18, but these passages seem almost irreconcilable with 1:5–2:2 and 5:16-17. If those born of God do not sin, why does claiming not to have sinned make God a liar? How can Christ be an atonement for sins that Christians cannot commit? What sins are there that Christians need to confess or pray about? There is nothing to show that the contradictory passages are speaking of different kinds of sin (Vitrano 1987; Whitacre 1982, 136-38; Rusam 1993, 140) or represent different kinds of perfectionism (Bogart 1977, 37-47, 135-36). Nor do 3:6, 9 seem to speak of a *possibility* of not sinning that the believer must realize (Bultmann 1973, 53; Marshall 1978, 182), or of a *process* of transformation toward sinlessness (Brown 1982, 431), or of a sinless *community* rather than sinless individuals (Perkins 1984, 38-42). The inconsistency is also not really a prefiguring of Luther's concept of the Christian as *simul justus et peccator,* righteous and sinner at the same time (Käsemann 1951, 306-9); the author does not bring the two opposing thoughts into this or any other clear relationship.

Other approaches get us little further. The present tense, used in 3:6, 9; 5:18, does generally imply continuous action, so that these verses could mean that Christians do not *habitually* sin, whereas the aorist tense in 2:1 could refer to single acts of sin into which they might lapse (du Preez 1975, 111; Painter 1986, 57). However, this does not account for the present tenses in 1:8 and 5:16, or the perfect in 1:10. In general, though few things are completely impossible for this writer, it seems unlikely that so significant a distinction would be expressed solely by this grammatical subtlety. One might also recall the author's practical purpose of encouraging the readers not to sin, a purpose that could make use of both of the conflicting kinds of statements (R. B. Edwards 1996, 102; see the comments on 1:7–2:1). Yet even if 1:5–2:2; 5:16-17 speak practically and 3:6, 9; 5:18 speak idealistically (Kubo 1969, 49-50; Dodd 1946, 80-81), they still must interact with, and so contradict, each other.

It is hard to say whether we have here a paradox that is not to be harmonized, a contradiction that represents the contradictoriness of Christian existence (Pratscher 1976, 272-73; Klauck 1991, 198), or simply the work of an author less concerned with clarity and consistency than we might wish. It is certainly important that the basis for the claim of sinlessness is the continuing and indwelling effect of divine birth (Brown 1982, 430-31). There is also some possibility that this claim derives ultimately from the opponents, since it so strongly resembles the position rejected in 1:8, 10 (Dodd 1946, 75-77; Swadling 1982, 206-8). If so, then the author would be agreeing with the opponents' contention that Christians, as children of God, are transformed people, but drawing a different implication from this truth. Note that the author does not claim that children of the devil *must* sin. It is the opponents for whom origins determine character or conduct. The author's point is not to derive conduct from origins, but *to demonstrate origins from conduct*. The thought of John 8:39-47 (and 5:19, 30) continues to underlie the ideas here: You can know who someone's parents are by the person's actions, for the child imitates the parent. The point is that God's children are not merely free of sin in principle, irrespective of their actions (a concept similar to some found in Gnosticism: *Adv. Haer.* 1.6.2-4). Rather, they must be so in practice. If indeed the divine "seed" abides in the believer, then it should manifest itself in freedom from actual deeds of sin. Because Jesus has "destroyed the works of the devil," those who believe in him are set free from those works (on all this, see Law 1914, 225-28).

For the opponents the question was, "Who is sinless?" and the answer was, "The children of God." For the author it was, "Who are the children of God?" and the answer was, "Those who do not sin"—that is, those who love one another (Painter 1986, 57). Once again, the opponents, in claiming sinlessness for believers in principle, may be superficially truer to the Gospel of John, where only those outside the believing community sin (since sin in John is always linked with refusal to believe in Jesus). However, it is the author who makes room for the other indispensable mark of Johannine Christianity, love for one another. In this way, of course, he also exposes the opponents as really being of the devil, despite their claim of perfection, and this seems to be his fundamental aim here.

Recognizing this aim does not wholly relieve the difficulty, but at least it lets us see the contradictory statements within their proper frames of reference. First John seeks to encourage the readers in two ways against the opponents' claim to be the sinless children of God. On the one hand, it offers the assurance of forgiveness to those who acknowledge their misdeeds within the framework of the community of love redeemed by the incarnate Christ (1:5–2:2; 5:16-17). On the other, it identifies God's true children as those who let the daily reality of their lives be transformed by this redemption in the concrete practice of righteousness, which is love (3:10). It is those who reject this visible transformation who reveal themselves to be deceivers and children of the devil.

◊ ◊ ◊ ◊

For 1 John, true eschatology, true Christology, and true ethics all go hand in hand. The elements of future eschatology in this section by no means displace the realized eschatology that is inherent in the Christian claim that Jesus is the Messiah. One aspect of this is seen in the continuity between the present nature of God's children and what will be revealed about them at the end: They *are* like Jesus, and *will be* like God (3:2-7; see also 2:6-8; 4:17). Therefore, those who hope to be like God then must be like Jesus now—they must live out the eschatological commandment of love, which thus characterizes both present and future. The opponents seem to have focused their realized eschatology on possession of the Spirit; our author focuses his on righteousness, that is, on love.

The language about "children of God" and "children of the devil" raises questions. Is it simply a metaphor for two opposed classes, like "children of light" and "children of darkness" (Luke 16:8; Eph 5:8; 1 Thess 5:5)? Or is the author thinking of offspring of God and the devil in a more literal sense, as two groups whose different origins unalterably determine their destinies? First John 2:19, in particular, seems to imply that kind of determinism. In a deterministic theology, however, people's actions may be irrelevant to their salvation, or may be predestined by their spiritual genesis. First John may not offer enough evidence for us to decide whether it is deterministic, but in any case it does not accept these conclusions. Rather, for 1 John it is precisely the opponents' deliberate lack of loving actions that reveals their identity as children of the devil.

On the other hand, the author's many-sided insistence on the imitation of Jesus and of God could suggest an attempt to justify oneself in God's sight by good works. Yet his claim that the children of God can be identified as those who do what is right is really the opposite of saying that "doing righteousness" is the way to *become* God's child. Moreover, the imitation of Christ that 1 John advocates means, not an artificial mimicry, but a life and a way of living that flow from the same source as Jesus', namely, the God who is love (see the concluding comments on 2:3-11).

Even so, however, it would be wrong to impose on 1 John a theory in which being God's child has nothing to do with being like God and Jesus. To be a child of God is to have been given God's love (3:1), but this love is given in order that its recipients may also love one another (4:7-11). Because they are God's children, believers resemble God and Jesus in their love. As God's children, however, they also deliberately seek to create this resemblance; that is why 1 John exhorts the readers to love one another. Neither a theory of meritorious action nor a theory of grace or predestination without reference to action is adequate to restate what 1 John says here and elsewhere. Our author cannot imagine achieving the status of child of God by one's own effort; but he also cannot imagine children of God who do not carry out acts of love toward one another (see further Webster 1986).

The author's preference for sinless practice over sinlessness in principle is part of the ethical realism noted earlier in connection with 1:5–2:2. Of course, most people will find that the claim that the children of God cannot sin conflicts with their own realistic experience. Yet the revelation and the example of Jesus and the abiding presence of God's Spirit do call forth a kind of sinlessness. To become a child of God is not an invisible or a theoretical transformation, nor are the identity and nature of God's children made known only at the end of time. They are present realities, both revealed and maintained in daily conduct. This conduct, moreover, is not a purely personal and individual holiness. Without brothers and sisters to love and be loved by, the real life of the child of God evaporates. In 1 John the whole question of sin and righteousness, of being or not being a child of God, comes down to loving one another concretely within a community, the family of God.

## LOVE AND HATRED (3:11-17)

The beginning of this section is clearly marked by the renewed appeal to what the readers have heard and known "from the beginning" (see 1:1; 2:7, 24). Its ending is somewhat more difficult to locate. Though 3:18 continues the theme of love, its fresh address "little children" and its close relation to verse 19 suggest that it makes a transition to the following section, and should be treated there. Verse 11 is a kind of header to the whole section (cf. 4:11). Verses 12-15 deal mainly with murder and hatred, and verses 16-17 with love and self-sacrifice. But verse 14 anticipates the theme of love, while verse 17 echoes that of harming one's brother or sister. The three references to knowing in verses 14-16 also help to hold the section together.

Partly because of the presence of "this is the message" both here and at 1:5, Raymond E. Brown (1982, 124-28) sees 3:11 as the beginning of the second half of 1 John, parallel to the second part of the Gospel of John (13–20). Certainly the theme of love announced in this verse dominates through the end of chapter 4. However, the opening "for" *(hoti)* links this section to the preceding one. So does its content, since, like 3:7-10, the new section contrasts love with the works of the devil, and 3:12, 15 take up the allusion to John 8:44 begun in 3:8. Such continuity is tolerable between two small sections, but hardly across the major boundary that Brown posits.

◊ ◊ ◊ ◊

The love for one another that was first introduced as a major theme in 2:7-11, and reintroduced at the end of 3:10, now becomes the primary topic. As before, it is contrasted with hatred; but here the contrast is more fully developed, continuing the pattern of dualistic oppositions from 2:28–3:10: love and hatred, self-sacrifice and murder, life and death, Jesus and Cain. Although these contrasts are presented in very general terms, the references to deceivers and false prophets in the surrounding material (3:7; 4:1) may suggest that the author had in mind the contrast between his party and the opponents as well. This will be worked out in the comments below.

Love is said to be expressed in giving one's own life for the sake of another, and hatred in the exact opposite, the taking of someone else's life. In a manner typical of parenetic writing, the author presents two examples to support this, one negative (Cain, v. 12) and the other positive (Jesus, v. 16). That Cain's deeds were evil and Abel's righteous was a commonplace of ancient Jewish and Christian interpretation, though there is not a hint of this in Genesis (see LXX Gen 4:7; Wis 10:3; Philo *Sacr.* 2-3; Philo *Det.* 32; Josephus *Ant.* 1 §53-54; *Tg. Ps.-J.* and *Tg. Neof.* Gen 4:8; Matt 23:35; Heb 11:4). That Cain was "from the evil one," that is, was a "child of the devil" (3:8, 10), may be a reference to Jewish legendary traditions in which the devil seduces Eve and fathers Cain, who becomes not only the first murderer but the first heretic (see Poly. *Phil.* 7.1; *Gos. Phil.* 61:5-10; Dahl 1964). The implication would be that Cain, in murdering his brother (Gen 4:1-16), imitated his father's conduct, since John 8:44 calls the devil "a murderer from the beginning."

Similarly to 1:5 (see also 2:7-11), the author reminds the readers of the message that they have heard from the beginning: the commandment to love one another (3:11; see further the concluding comments on this section). As before, "from the beginning" refers to the Johannine tradition, no doubt specifically to John 13:34-35; 15:12, 17. The appeal to tradition is reinforced by several other allusions to the Fourth Gospel. The murderous Cain as "from the evil one" (3:12), and the term "murderer" itself (3:15), continue the reference to John 8:37-47 begun in 3:8. The passage from death to life (3:14) is an allusion to John 5:24 (see also 8:51). Beyond this, we may compare Cain's "evil deeds" (3:12) with John 3:19-21; 7:7; the world's hatred of Christians (3:13) with John 15:18-20; 17:14; and the laying down of one's life (3:16) with John 15:13 (see also 10:11-18). In John, the devil appears primarily in connection with Jesus' betrayal and death (6:70; 8:39-47; 12:31-32; 13:2; 14:30-31), and this tradition too may be in the background of our author's ascription of hatred and murder to the children of the devil and love and life-giving to the children of God.

These allusions are made, not to assert the authority of the tradition as such, but to draw out its implications in the dispute with the opponents over its meaning, thus demonstrating who truly represents Johannine Christianity. Those who do evil, like Cain, are of the evil one; those who do right are like the righteous one, Jesus (3:7-10). According to the Fourth Gospel (see the references above), people who rejected Jesus did so because their deeds were evil. The world hated him for exposing its evil deeds, and was ready to kill him because it refused his word; and this hatred was directed at his disciples also. What was true of Abel, of Jesus, and of Jesus' disciples, then, is also true of the readers: the world hates them because of their righteous deeds, that is, because of their acts of love (3:10). These acts certify that they have heard the word of Jesus, and so have passed from the realm of the world and death to that of God and eternal life.

The use of "brothers and sisters" *(adelphoi)* as a direct address to the readers, common in Paul, is found only in 3:13 in the Johannine epistles. The author seems to be playing on the reference to Cain's fratricide in the preceding verse: The readers also are "brothers and sisters" endangered by treachery. The implication is that, while the author wants to maintain a faithful sibling relationship with them, the opponents offer a hatred like that of the world itself (see 4:5). Verse 15 then makes explicit the symbolic meaning of the example of Cain: the murderer is anyone who hates a brother or sister (cf. *T. Benj.* 7:5). This seems, at first glance, a very sweeping statement. While it is typical of the absoluteness of Johannine dualism, however, it is also strikingly reminiscent of Matt 5:21-22. Whether or not the author was aware of that saying, he follows the same pattern of reducing an ethical issue to its most basic form. Thus, it is not necessary to suppose that the opponents posed an actual mortal danger to other Christians. Their hatred is simply their failure to love, which will be further explicated in verse 17.

The pronoun "we" at the beginning of verse 14 includes both author and readers, and so serves to draw the readers onto the author's side. It is also emphatic, hinting that there are others who make this claim to life but without the proper basis: they do not love, and so they abide in death. The opponents, with their very high Christology, may also have claimed to heed the word of Christ (John 5:24), meaning the christological proclamation of the One who came down from heaven. In this they would have correctly understood the primary meaning of the sayings about the "word" of Jesus in the Fourth Gospel. For 1 John, however, the word to be kept is the commandment to love one another (v. 11); or rather, it is this commandment united with christological faith (3:23). Those who do not love do not truly believe in Jesus, who revealed the God who is love (4:7-11). In this sin the opponents die (John 8:21, 24), and so "abide in death." Thus, it is the author and his followers who are the authentically Johannine Christians, the ones on the right side of the dualism of life and death and the ones who truly embody the realized eschatology that claims already to possess eternal life.

By saying that the readers "know" that no murderer has eternal life, the author implies that this was part of the tradition familiar to them, as in verse 14. Since there is nothing similar to this in the Gospel of John, the reference may be to common early Christian ethical instruction, which included murder in lists of vices that lead to the loss of eternal life (Rom 1:28-32; Rev 21:8; 22:14-15). Here as elsewhere, 1 John shows awareness of Christian traditions outside the Johannine sphere.

After all the talk of murder and hatred, the author in verse 16 turns back to love, and to Jesus its cardinal exemplar. The verse begins with a discernment formula (see the comments on 2:3). The sense of continuity implied in the Greek perfect tense verb "we have known" (NRSV: "we know") is underscored by one further appeal to Johannine tradition. The expression "to lay down one's life" is found only in this verse and in John 10:11-18; 15:13 in the New Testament. It removes any possible doubt about whether the love under discussion is a matter of words and feelings only, or of action. The believers' long-held knowledge is thus not just a comforting doctrine. It is knowledge with a point, the point being the imitation of Jesus' love, the theme just explored so thoroughly in 2:28–3:10. As in similar contexts, we find the verb "ought" (2:6; 4:11; see also John 13:14); and the pronoun *ekeinos*, "he," is used for Jesus (see the comments on 2:3-6). The reference to the laying down of lives is not necessarily metaphorical or hyperbolic. Yet there is no mention of persecution in 1 John, and the author may well be interpreting John 15:12-13 in a new, less dangerous situation.

Verse 17, in fact, suggests one specific understanding of the laying down of one's life, perhaps actually the most important one in the community's present situation: help for brothers and sisters in economic need. This community, like other early Christian groups, may have included a mixture of social levels (cf. 1 Cor 11:20-22; Jas 2:15-16), which would have challenged the better-off members to make reality of the traditional Johannine language of love. It is possible that the opponents comprised mainly such people, and that their thought was rooted more in an individualistic spirituality than in Jewish eschatology, with its strong theme of hope for economic and social justice. Their "spiritual" Christology, which placed little value on the physical humanity of Jesus, may have led them to conclude that material need was not a matter of spiritual concern. At any rate, when they withdrew from fellowship with the rest of the community, they may also have refused to aid its poor members. There is an interesting parallel in Ign. *Smyrn.* 6.2, where Docetists are accused of caring nothing for love and of neglecting widows, orphans, prisoners, and the poor.

"Goods," or "wealth," is the same word as in 2:16, *bios* (see the comments there). Though its association with the world may give it some negative coloring, it is not treated here as something essentially bad. Its one right use, however, is for the good of brothers and sisters in need. As in 2:15-17, it is not the things in the world themselves that are evil, but human attitudes toward them. Yet what is truly contrary to the love of God is not simply an attitude but the actions that result from it (3:18). There is no point in claiming to have a Christian attitude toward our possessions if we continue to possess them while our sisters and brothers are in need.

Feelings are not irrelevant to acts of love, however. The NRSV's rather anemic "refuses help" translates "closes off one's *splagchna*," literally "intestines," which were regarded as the seat of compassion. In English, we would say "heart." The vivid metaphor reflects an obvious psychological truth: People must shut off their inner selves, the emotions of care and concern and the bodily sensations that accompany them, in order to maintain an indifference to others in need. Only when they have walled themselves off emotionally can they wall themselves off theologically and materially as well.

As in 2:5, 15 (see the comments there), it is a difficult question whether "the love of God" means "God's love" (subjective genitive; thus NRSV) or "love for God" (objective genitive). The parallel in 4:20-21 favors the latter. Yet the former is even more strongly supported by 4:7-18, which is closer to the context here: God loves us, and it is that love of God active in us that enables and requires us to love one another (3:16). God's love, which we have experienced in Christ's sacrifice of himself for us, dwells actively in us as we give up what we have for one another; it is indeed God's love for our brothers and sisters working itself out through us.

◊ ◊ ◊ ◊

The repetition of "this is the message" in 1:5 and 3:11 suggests that the two messages, "God is light" and "love one another," are essentially equivalent for this author. Elsewhere in 1 John, love is a commandment; here it is the "message," *aggelia*, a term closely related to *euaggelion,* "gospel, good news." For 1 John, the Christian message or news is that we are to love one another, a love made known in the self-sacrifice of the Son of God. The message about Jesus cannot be separated from the message that God's children love one another; they are the same message. For 1 John, *love is not law but gospel,* the glad tidings of what God has made possible for human beings. The "indicative" of salvation and the "imperative" of ethics are truly one; "faith" and "works" interpenetrate so that neither one is independent of the other. Doing is not only the measure of believing, it *is* believing.

In its Johannine form, of course, this love is for "brothers and sisters," that is, for other Christians (see the comments on 2:3-11). If this is a narrowing of love's scope, it brings a corresponding increase in its intensity. First John reflects the central mystery of Christian ethics: the way to pass from death to life is to give up one's life in love; refusing to give up one's life for others is abiding in death. This theme is certainly Johannine (John 12:24-26; 15:12-13), but its origin is in the teaching of Jesus himself (Mark 8:34-37; 10:29-31; Matt 10:38-39; Luke 14:26-27; 17:33). However problematic 1 John may be in other respects, it represents a Christianity in which both community and witness were strong enough to render this language plausible. And if life itself was not held too dear to offer to one's sisters and brothers, how much less a mere matter of "the world's goods"?

## CONFIDENCE TOWARD GOD (3:18-24)

First John 3:18 is an example of what Raymond E. Brown (1982, 119) calls a "hinge" verse. It continues the theme of love from verses 11-17; yet the address "little children" signals the beginning of a new section. The internal coherence of 3:18-24 is rather limited, consisting mainly of a series of verbal connections, initiated by the repetition of "truth" in verses 18, 19. Verses 19-22, though in part very difficult to follow, clearly belong together, their topic being Christians' confidence before God due to their keeping of the commandments. Verses 23-24 again seem to be a "hinge." They continue the subject of keeping the commandments, but they also announce the most prominent themes of chapters 4 and 5: right Christology, love, abiding, and the Spirit. Indeed, these verses serve as the introduction to 4:1-6 (on Christology) and 4:7-18 (on love).

◊ ◊ ◊ ◊

Verse 18 sums up the concern of verses 16-17, that love be a matter of deeds. "Word" and "action" (or "deed"; Greek *logos* and *ergon*) make up a formula widespread in Greek literature. The contrast of mere words with truth and deed is reminiscent of the way Cynic philosophers used this formula (Merritt 1993, 61-69). However, though "in truth" ordinarily means just "truly," in a Johannine context it takes on a deeper resonance. Loving action is not self-generated but flows from the truth, that is, from the divine reality to which those who love belong (v. 19; cf. "doing the truth" in 1:6, and the comments there).

First John 3:19-20 is one of the most obscure sentences in the New Testament. In the first place, "by this" generally points forward in 1 John, but here there is really nothing to which it could point. Instead, it must point backward to loving in truth, which assures us that we are of the truth. (On this discernment formula, see the comments on 2:3.) The verb *peisomen* should mean "we shall convince"; but commentators often cite evidence for "we shall pacify" or "reassure" (NRSV). In the following clauses we find *hoti* (either "that" or "because"), *ean* (normally "if"), and another *hoti*. It is the presence of two *hoti*s that lies at the root of the problem (compare the comments on 5:9). Translated literally, and with all the ambiguities displayed, the Greek runs, "In this we shall know that we are of the truth, and before him we shall convince/reassure our heart that/because, if the heart condemns us, that/because God is greater than our heart and knows everything."

The most common solution is to translate *peisomen* "reassure"; to reinterpret *hoti ean* as *ho ti an*, "in whatever case, whenever"; and to translate the second *hoti* "because" or "for" (e.g, NRSV, NIV, NAB, REB; Brooke 1912, 100; Marshall 1978, 197 n. 4; Schnackenburg 1992, 185). However, the evidence that *peisomen* can mean "reassure" is weak, as is the evidence for this adverbial usage of *ho ti an* (which is also in the wrong case to be the object of "condemn" [Boyer 1988, 254]). Some, therefore, consider the second *hoti* redundant, either as simply resuming the first or as a grammatical error. This yields either "we shall reassure our heart because, if our heart condemns us, God is greater . . . " (cf. the KJV); or (more naturally) "we shall convince our heart that, if our heart condemns us, God is greater . . ." (cf. the NEB; and see, e.g., Houlden 1973, 102; Brown 1982, 457-58). First John does not use a resumptive *hoti* in comparable passages elsewhere (3:2; 5:14); however, it seems more plausible that the author has violated his usual practice in this regard than that he has created virtually unparalleled usages of *peisomen* and *ho ti an*. The translation adopted by Houlden, Brown, and others is probably correct.

The intent of verses 19-20 is evidently to be reassuring, but, because the wording is so unclear, it scarcely succeeds: for most of Christian history this sentence has been regarded as a stern warning (Brown 1982, 459). The thought that God knows everything does often imply a warning that people cannot escape divine judgment (e.g., Ps 7:9; 139; Prov 15:3, 11; Jer 20:12; Heb 4:12-13). Sometimes, though, we find the sense that God takes cognizance of both good and evil, and so will judge the good-hearted positively (1 Sam 16:7; 1 Chr 28:9; Acts 1:24-25; 15:8; 1 Cor 4:5; note also John 21:17). Elsewhere in 1 John, statements about divine judgment are generally encouraging for those who imitate Christ in acts of love (2:28–3:3; 4:17-18; see also 2:1-2, 17). Since this sentence begins with the assurance that those who love actively are "from the truth," it must also be meant as encouragement, as nearly all modern commentators agree. Certain that they are of the truth, those who love can convince their troubled hearts that God knows everything—that is, that God knows precisely that they are of the truth. God, being greater than our hearts, is greater even than what our hearts think of God, and is faithful to forgive (1:9) without the compulsive reparations that a guilty heart may demand (Pratscher 1976, 278-81).

If this interpretation is generally correct, then verses 21-22 are probably not an alternative to verses 19-20 but their continuation. If we convince our heart that God knows better and will not condemn us, *then* our heart also will no longer condemn us, and we can feel perfectly confident in prayer. In fact, verse 22*b* ties the whole together as a single thought by offering the same reason for confidence as verses 18-19: keeping the commandment of love. At the same time, by reintroducing the term "commandment" for the first time since 2:7-8, it leads into verses 23-24.

The confidence expressed here (and in 5:14-15) is obviously different from the eschatological confidence of 2:28, though the same term, *parrēsia*, is used. Confidence in asking and receiving is part of the Johannine tradition (John 16:23-27), derived ultimately from the teaching of Jesus (Matt 7:7-8; Luke 11:9-10; Mark 11:24). The connection with keeping the commandments seems specifically based on John 15:7-17. The Fourth Gospel, however, avoids the flat impression of obedience and reward that this passage makes; as elsewhere, the epistles lack the Gospel's subtlety.

In John, the disciples are to make their requests to Jesus, or in Jesus' name; here Christians pray directly to God. Similarly, according to verse 24 Christians themselves abide in God, whereas in the Fourth Gospel Jesus always stands as intermediary between the two (see the comments on 2:6). In John, it is the keeping of Jesus' commandments that allows believers to receive the Spirit and to have Jesus dwelling in them (14:15-24); here God is the giver of the commandments. Thus, here as elsewhere 1 John reduces the mediating role of Jesus and attributes things to God that the Gospel attributes to Jesus (see the introduction). On the other hand, in the Gospel of John it is Jesus who always does what pleases God and keeps God's commandments (8:29, 55; 12:49-50; 14:30-31), particularly the commandment to give up his life in love (10:17-18; 15:10-13); and it is Jesus whom God always hears (John 11:22, 42). Christians who, in obedience to God, keep this same commandment of love thus imitate the Johannine Jesus (1 John 3:16), and, like him, they are heard by God.

Verses 23-24 contain in a nutshell the themes that pervade 1 John. They give a full and clear statement of what the author considers essential. The repetition of "commandment" at the beginning and the end of verse 23 (the NRSV renders the second "commanded") seems to incorporate both belief and love in a single commandment. Urban C. von Wahlde (1990, 52-53), however, makes a good case on the basis of chiastic structure that while the plural "commandments" in verses 22, 24 refer to God's commandments in general, each of the singulars in verse 23 refers to only one commandment, first belief and then love. This justifies the repetition of "commandment"; yet even if there are two commandments, the fundamental conviction of 1 John is that they are a unity and that neither can be maintained without the other.

There is a striking similarity between these commandments and the two that, according to Mark 12:28-34, Jesus posited as the greatest in the law. It is conceivable that our author was aware of that tradition (see the comments on 4:21). However, these two commandments are also a distillation of the message of the Gospel of John, and each has a characteristically Johannine turn (von Wahlde 1990, 239-44). In the second commandment, love is not for "your neighbor" in general, but for "one another" within the Christian community (see the comments on 2:3-11). The first commandment has as its object not God but Jesus, and speaks not of love but of belief, equivalent to "confession" in 2:22-23; 4:2-3, 15; 2 John 7. Christological confession held a profoundly important place in the history and consciousness of the Johannine community, which had both asserted and suffered for a fully articulated and openly confessed faith in Jesus in former times (John 9:22; 12:42; see Rensberger 1988, 39-41, 45-48). The author appeals to this history by means of the formulation here. To "*believe* in the *name* of his *Son Jesus Christ*" comprises all the elements vital for Johannine Christology "from the beginning" (see John 11:27; 20:31; also 1 John 5:1, 4-5, 10, 13), including the importance of Jesus' name (John 1:12; 2:23; 3:18; see the comments on 2:12). For 1 John, such belief means maintaining the full incarnational Christology that the opponents have called into question.

Thus paired, these two commandments present a distinctively Johannine view of what is essential to Christianity. As implied in the comments on 3:17, not only each commandment individually but their association with each other may be significant in relation to the opponents. The refusal of the latter to identify the human Jesus as the divine Christ and Son may have involved a general devaluation of the earthly human life in which love is lived out. Likewise, they may not have seen in Jesus' own humanity a model of love for Christians to follow. For 1 John this means, not a fresh interpretation, but simply a betrayal of Johannine tradition.

The language of mutual indwelling in verse 24 is also characteristically Johannine. However, as noted above, the abiding of God *directly* in Christians and they in God goes beyond anything that is said in the Gospel of John. Criteria other than the Spirit for discerning this abiding, all closely related to the commandments in verse 23, are given in 2:5-6, 24; 3:6; 4:12-16. (On the discernment formula itself, see the comments on 2:3.) How the presence of the Spirit can be detected is not stated, but in Johannine thought the Spirit functions mainly in teaching (John 14:25-26; 16:12-15; see the comments on 2:20, 27). In the context of a controversy over christological teaching, however, even the Spirit is submitted to a christological criterion in 4:1-6. There is thus at least some truth to Raymond E. Brown's assertion that the way in which the Spirit verifies that Christians abide in God is their profession of the true Christology (1982, 483-84). Although the possession of the Spirit and mutual abiding with God are interior events, they are validated by means that are not individualistic or esoteric but thoroughly public: confession of faith and love for one another.

◊ ◊ ◊ ◊

Many will feel that the automatic receiving of what one asks for in prayer (v. 22) does not accord with their experience. Yet this statement expresses a consistent theme of the New Testament, and indeed of the Bible as a whole. It belongs to that sense of deep and reliant trust in God that is the basic meaning of "faith" in biblical language, a living relationship and not simply a "belief system." At least equally as troubling, perhaps, is the implication that such answering of prayer is a reward for obedience. The joining of answered prayer to righteousness is also common in the Bible, Judaism, and early Christianity (e.g., Job 22:21-27; Philo *Praem.* 84; Jas 5:16; *2 Clem.* 15.3-5; contrast *Herm. Man.* 9.1-4). Raymond E. Brown, however, points out that the covenant relationship of love between Christians and God, and the unity of wills brought about by living faithfully within that relationship, provides another perspective than that of mere reward (1982, 479-80). To live in fidelity to and dependence on God's will is neither to keep a checklist of rules nor to enjoy uninterrupted prosperity. It is to "abide in God," and so to live with no other source of security in the world, to enter fully into the risk of turning away from material and social safety to rely on God alone, a risk that the Johannine community knew from experience (John 15:18-25; 16:33; 17:11-19). It is within this context of trust, risk-filled faithfulness, and mutual love that 1 John's assertions about prayer are made.

The fact that belief and love are presented as *commandments* in the Johannine writings can also be troublesome. Is such faith really still a relationship, or has it become merely dogmatic? How can God command us what to feel about people? We cannot produce genuine belief or genuine feelings at anyone's command, even God's. One does, in fact, sense a rudimentary dogmatism already in the Fourth Gospel's insistence on particular beliefs about Jesus (Käsemann 1968, 23-26 and passim), a dogmatism that becomes even stronger in 1 and 2 John. To be sure, these texts represent responses to specific challenges to christological belief, and it is always the content and not the form of belief that is significant for them. Even 1 John does not elaborate a system of doctrine, or hint that one is necessary. Rather, it focuses on one essential thing: recognizing that in Jesus of Nazareth, God not only sent the world a Messiah, but encountered the world in a revelation of divine reality. Yet there is no mistaking that for the Johannine Gospel and epistles this recognition *is* a requirement; for how can one be in a relationship with God without acknowledging the self-revelation that God has made?

As for love, perhaps what really matters is not that love is a commandment but that the commandment is *love,* rather than ritual purity or moral perfection. Most important, as noted in the comments on 3:11-17, for 1 John love is not law but gospel. Furthermore, in 1 John as elsewhere in the New Testament, love is more than feeling; it is action. The commandment is not an imperious demand to summon up warm feelings, but a gracious offer of a way of living in openness to seeing and meeting the needs of others. Nor is love a requirement chosen arbitrarily; rather, it is the essence of the very self-revelation of God that is the object of faith (4:8, 16).

These two commandments, of belief in Jesus and of love for one another, are essential Christianity for 1 John. Without them, there is nothing deserving of that name. New developments may perhaps elaborate on them, but they may not contradict them, as the spiritual "advances" of the opponents seem to have done. Neither has priority over the other; indeed, neither is conceivable without the other. Christian love is not simply normal human affection or even self-sacrificing devotion, but arises from the eschatological revelation of what God is in Jesus Christ. One can no more accept that revelation without accepting this life of love, however, than one could be alive without breathing.

## TESTING THE SPIRITS (4:1-6)

This brief section takes up the first of the two commandments introduced in 3:23, belief in Jesus; the next section (4:7-18) will take up the second commandment, love for one another. The discussion of the Spirit here also prepares for the repetition of 3:24*b* in 4:13. Within the present section, verses 1-3 deal with the Spirit of God and the spirit of antichrist, and verses 4-6 correspondingly with people who are of God and people who are of the world, ending with a final statement on the spirits, which makes an inclusion that rounds off the section.

◊ ◊ ◊ ◊

There is no reason to think that the language of "false prophets" and the references to spirits are merely formal (v. 1), though they are rooted in traditional eschatological expectations. Evidently some in the community, including the opponents, were claiming to speak under the influence of the Holy Spirit. The author does not mention the kind of phenomena usually considered "charismatic"; but in the Johannine tradition, teaching as such is charismatic (John 14:26; 16:13; see the comments on 1 John 2:20, 27). Early Christian prophecy in general did not mean just ecstatic predictions of the future. It also included exhortation and teaching, which could be given as inspired utterances (1 Cor 14:1-6, 22-25; Rev 2:20; 10:11; note "teachers" in the lists in Rom 12:6-8; 1 Cor 12:28-30; Eph 4:11). First John can therefore speak of false teachers as false prophets (though the Gospel of John, unlike many other NT writings, never calls Christians "prophets"). Claims of inspiration played a central role in early Christianity. The question for the Johannine community was whether such teachers really were inspired by the Spirit of God (3:24).

New religious movements often experience such controversies. Deceivers and false prophets, messiahs, and teachers are mentioned in Matt 24:11; Mark 13:5-6, 21-22; 1 Tim 4:1; 2 Pet 2:1; Rev 12:9; 13:11-15; 16:13-14; 19:20; 20:10; *Did.* 16.4. Many of these are eschatological, and so are related to the antichrist (v. 3; see the comments on 2:18-27, and see also 2 John 7). First Thessalonians 5:19-22 speaks of testing prophecies and Rev 2:2 of testing self-proclaimed apostles, without mentioning criteria. In Matt 7:15-23; *Did.* 11.3-12; *Herm. Man.* 11.7-16, the test for false prophets is conduct; there is a doctrinal test for teachers in *Did.* 11.1-2. A test of spirits is also offered in 1 Cor 12:3, and since it too concerns confession of Jesus it is at least conceivable that a similar issue was involved (Painter 1986, 65). (The examination of members' spirits at Qumran is something different, however.)

The origin of all such tests in the biblical tradition is the testing of prophets in Deut 13:1-5; 18:20-22, where the main criterion is that false prophets speak in the name of gods not previously known. First John's call to resist the antichrists by remaining in the christological tradition known "from the beginning" (2:22-24) and the reference to idols in 5:21 resemble this ancient criterion. The insistence on love for one another is more like the tests of conduct found in other early Christian texts, but it is not explicitly connected with claims to the Spirit.

If a spirit is not "from God," one might expect it to be "from the devil." Instead, however, we find "the antichrist," "the world," and "error" (or "deceit"). Since "the one who is in the world" most likely means the evil one, however (see 5:19), the devil probably is in fact "the spirit of the antichrist" (v. 3). It is not absolutely clear whether the author thinks of only one such spirit inspiring the opponents, or of various spirits directed by the devil. That there are "many" false prophets echoes the "many" antichrists of 2:18. (Of course, there is only one Spirit of God, which causes a lack of symmetry.) The statement that the false prophets have "gone out" into the world may mean only that they have "come forth" or "appeared," not that they have left the Johannine group, despite the similarity to 2:19. Even so, their association with "the world" in verses 4-5 may suggest a negative connotation already in verse 1.

First John 4:2 presents the author's most direct statement of the christological point at issue. (On "by this you know," see the comments on 2:3; on the significance of confessing Christ in Johannine history, see the comments on 3:23.) Unfortunately, it is so ambiguous that we must once again consider several possible interpretations, and the choice will significantly affect our overall understanding of 1 John. The Greek reads literally "every spirit that confesses Jesus Christ having come in flesh is from God." At first glance, this closely resembles the NRSV's "confesses that Jesus Christ has come in the flesh" (similarly NIV, REB). However, to stress simply *that* Jesus Christ has come in flesh would probably require an infinitive in the Greek. The use of the participle "having come" places more emphasis on the *person* who has come (Lieu 1981, 219; Lieu 1991, 75).

The grammar allows three other possible translations: (a) "confesses *Jesus Christ as having come* in the flesh"; (b) the confession of the entire *concept* "Jesus Christ come in the flesh"; and (c) "confesses *Jesus as Christ* who has come in the flesh" (cf. John 9:22; Rom 10:9). Commentators who prefer (c) argue that this ambiguous sentence should be interpreted by the unambiguous formulas in 2:22; 4:15; 5:1, 5, which, together with 4:3, suggest that *Jesus* is to be confessed as the incarnate Messiah (Miranda 1977, 158-59; Law 1914, 93-95; Houlden 1973, 107). However, usage elsewhere in 1 John (note especially 3:23) suggests that "Jesus Christ" is to be taken together as a compound name. Raymond E. Brown rightly notes how the lack of "is" distinguishes this formula from the others cited above, and he therefore prefers (b) (1982, 493; also Westcott 1892, 141; Brooke 1912, 108-9; Smalley 1984, 222). Comparison with 5:6, however, suggests that the confession is about the salvific *coming* of Jesus Christ. Thus, (a) is probably correct (de Boer 1991, 333-37; Klauck 1991, 228; Schnackenburg 1992, 200).

Even so, the combination "Jesus Christ" does recall the other confessions where the identity of the human Jesus with the divine Christ, the Son of God, is at issue (see the comments on 2:22). First John 4:2 also promotes this identity, but primarily asserts the importance of this one person as "having come in flesh" (AT), that is, as having acted for salvation through concrete human existence. "Jesus" in verse 3, though essentially an abbreviation for the formula in verse 2, reminds us that the human Jesus was the central issue. The opponents apparently did not deny the *reality* of this human being, and thus were not "Docetists" in the technical sense (see the introduction). Nevertheless, precisely because Jesus' humanity was physical, "flesh," they seem to have denied its *value* for salvation, and instead placed all emphasis on the divine Christ and the revelation he brought. They may even have understood John 1:14 with an emphasis on this divine "glory" (Brown 1982, 75-78).

However one translates verse 2, what it calls for is the confession not of a proposition, but of a person, "not of the fact of the Incarnation, but of the Incarnate Christ" (Brooke 1912, 109). The opponents have not simply refused assent to a dogmatic formula; they have misunderstood the identity of the one in whom the love of God was revealed, and so failed to understand that love itself. The use of the perfect tense "having come" adds to the impression that not just the fact of the Incarnation but its enduring significance was at issue: Jesus Christ not only was, but still *is*, the Incarnate One (cf. the present tense in 2 John 7).

There is one further difficulty here. All Greek manuscripts read "does not confess Jesus" in verse 3. There is some evidence in Latin translations and early Christian writers, however, for the reading "*separates* (or destroys) Jesus." Some commentators accept this, suggesting that copyists replaced this unusual and difficult reading with the more obvious "does not confess" (Brown 1982, 494-96;

Schnackenburg 1992, 201-2). The manuscript evidence is decisive, however; "separates Jesus" was probably created as a vivid expression for use in second-century christological debates (Ehrman 1988; Westcott 1892, 163-66; Brooke 1912, 111-14).

"The world" in verses 4-6 is no longer neutral, as in verses 1-3, but has its fully Johannine sense of that which is opposed to God and has always opposed the Johannine community (see the comments on 2:15-17). The contrast between God and the world also serves to separate the readers from the opponents and to identify them with the author. The latter is "from God," but so are the readers, who therefore must already make the christological confession specified in verse 2. In 2:12-14, they were congratulated for having conquered "the evil one," that is, "the one who is in the world" (see 5:19). In a rather bold stroke, the author now says it is the *opponents* whom they have conquered. The opponents' Christology marks them as not from God, and so they must be "from the world." "We [the author and his party] are from God"; those who are from God can be discerned by whether they agree with "us," and so "we [the author and the readers!] know" true spirits from false (v. 6). By such rhetorical means, the author seeks to draw the readers onto his side, crediting them with success in his goal of defeating the opponents.

This type of appeal is useful within a circle where all are agreed, but it has obvious limitations when trying to convince the genuinely undecided. In the Gospel of John it is only those who listen to Jesus who are of God (John 5:37-38; 6:45; 8:42-47). By identifying the message of 1 John with that of Jesus in the Gospel (beginning already in the prologue), our author simultaneously identifies his opponents with Jesus' opponents. This is a damning accusation; but in a dispute over the true interpretation of Johannine tradition, the claim to true understanding of the Johannine Jesus is precisely the point at issue. Such an aggressive begging of the question could conceivably do more harm than good, offending the readers' sense of integrity and causing them to turn to the opponents.

Of course, the opponents may also have claimed to be hostile to the world; it was, after all, they who devalued the "flesh" of Jesus. Therefore, to demonstrate that they really are "from the world," the author points out that "the world listens to them" (v. 5), which probably means that they were engaged in a successful mission to non-Christians. It would be too much to say that the author himself was no longer interested in mission (see 1 John 2:2; 4:14; 3 John 5-8). However, even if the sense is simply that the opponents' mission was more successful than the author's, their success as such seems to be treated negatively. Their attractiveness to the world is not an unambiguous sign of faithfulness to God's mission, but calls their means into question: "what they say is from the world."

"Spirit of truth" (v. 6) is a typical Johannine epithet for the Holy Spirit (John 14:17; 15:26; 16:13; note also 4:23-24; 1 John 2:27; 5:6). The term is also known from Qumran, though in a somewhat different sense (1QS 3:18-19; 4:21, 23). "Spirit of deceit" (AT) as its opposite may be an innovation of 1 John (the Qumran texts speak of the "spirit of wickedness"), although the frequent appearance of similar terms in the *Testaments of the Twelve Patriarchs* (e.g., *T. Reub.* 2.1; *T. Jud.* 14.8; 20.1-5 [opposed to the spirit of truth]; *T. Iss.* 4.4) may indicate that it was known in sectarian Judaism. The phrase may refer to the devil or to spirits sent from the devil to inspire the opponents. (The NRSV's "spirit of error" is potentially misleading; the author considers the opponents' teaching not just mistaken but deceptive [Gk. *planē*].) Placing the Holy Spirit over against the "spirit of deceit" is somewhat odd, the result of inserting "Spirit of truth" into a dualistic framework. It seems unlikely, however, that a merely human "spirit" or the like is in view; "Spirit of God" in 4:2 is unambiguous (note also 3:24; 4:13). The author and his opponents are contesting for the "authentic" Johannine tradition, including the legitimate testimony of the Spirit of truth (5:6-8). The terminology here must surely echo that tradition, even if the author's dualism leads the interpretation of the tradition in an unexpected direction.

◊ ◊ ◊ ◊

First John 4:2 seems to emphasize Jesus Christ as having carried out the work of salvation in human life. Thus, whether or not we accept José Porfirio Miranda's reading of this verse, his insistence on the social significance of Johannine Christology is appropriate

(1977, 176, 182-200). If the messiahship of Jesus was a material human event, "in the flesh," then it provides both a basis and a mandate for Christians' lives to be meaningful in material human reality, both individual and social. This is one major reason why Christology and the love commandment are so inseparable in 1 John: Jesus' truly human life provides both the source and the model for his followers' lives.

What the opponents seem to have denied was not the reality of Jesus' human nature but its salvific value. They may have held that it was not the flesh of the human Jesus that brought salvation, but the fact that the Son of God came down from heaven and revealed his glory, and the glory of God. The questions involved were not only christological but soteriological. Can human beings be saved only by one who does not share their flesh and all its weaknesses; or only by one who precisely does own their nature and experience their pain and longing? Christianity ultimately decided in favor of the latter, with the aid of writings such as 1 John, Hebrews, and the synoptic Gospels in its New Testament canon. At this early date, however, the issue was still very much open.

The opponents' position was probably affected by the dualism of hellenistic culture, and therefore it presents an early instance of a perpetual problem in Christian mission, the extent to which the presentation of the gospel can be adapted to local cultures. The hellenism of the eastern Mediterranean was one such local culture, and the New Testament writings exemplify in various ways both adaptation to it (most notably the Gospel of John itself) and critique of adaptations considered too extreme (e.g, 2 Corinthians and Colossians). The opponents may have thought that their numerical success confirmed the validity and divine inspiration of their christological message. Our author feared that they were in danger of losing the truly Christian character of the gospel altogether. The point he makes is that if those who hear the message are of God, they will listen to the gospel of the Incarnation. It is not open to the evangelist to sugarcoat the message with a popular spirituality that might cut it loose from the contingent and everyday nature—the flesh—of human life, both Jesus' and our own.

# GOD IS LOVE (4:7-18)

This section takes up the second commandment introduced in
3:23, loving one another. First John 4:1-6 had treated the christological commandment, and the repetition of "from God" and
"knows God" connects verse 7 to verse 6. The section may be
divided into two units, verses 7-10 and verses 11-18, each introduced by "beloved." Within the latter unit there are two brief
discussions set up by verse 12: "God abides in us" (AT) establishes
the topic of verses 13-16, and "his love is perfected in us" does the
same for verses 17-18. (The former is obscured in the NRSV by the
translation "live" rather than "abide" for *menō* in v. 12.) Each of
these two discussions begins with the discernment formula "by/in
this" (vv. 13, 17; others are in vv. 9, 10; see the comments on 2:3).

Most English translations and commentaries do not consider
verses 11-18 a unit, dividing verse 16 in the middle instead, and
treating verse 16*b* as the beginning of a new unit (e.g., NRSV, NIV,
NAB; Brooke 1912, 122; Brown 1982, 545). New units, however,
really begin at 4:7, 11, and 19, all of which express the same theme,
that Christians should love because of God's love. In the unit
beginning with verse 11, after verse 12 has established the topic of
abiding, verses 13-16 present a carefully ordered discussion of it
(analyzed in the commentary below; see also Haas, de Jonge, and
Swellengrebel 1972, 111). By returning to love as the criterion for
abiding, verse 16*b* forms an inclusion with verse 12, confirming
both the unity of verses 13-16 and their structural dependence
(along with vv. 17-18) on verse 12.

◊ ◊ ◊ ◊

This section bases the requirement to love not on a commandment (3:23) but on the very nature of God. The section also
combines, clarifies, and makes more explicit other themes begun
earlier, and so forms as much of a climax as 1 John's loose structure
allows. These themes all relate to the connection between relationship with God and loving one another (2:3-11; 2:28–3:10). If love
is from God, then the people who are from God (2:29; 3:9-10;
4:1-6) should also love one another. Christians' love is thus a *result*

of their being from God, not the cause of it. Yet that is not what 1 John emphasizes, and as elsewhere the two are so closely intertwined that neither of them is absolutely independent of the other (see the concluding comments on 2:28–3:10).

Also as elsewhere, love is restricted to "one another" within the Christian community (see the comments on 2:3-11). Taken in isolation, the wording of verse 7 might suggest that even non-Christians who truly love know God and are born of God. That, however, is not our author's concern. Rather, the love in question was revealed in the eschatological sending of the Son of God (vv. 9-10, 14-16), and belief in this sending, with the love that it entails, defines Christianity for 1 John. The author is also interested in those who do not love, however, that is, the opponents. Comparison of verse 8 with 3:1 shows that they are once again being put on the same level as the world.

The claim that God is love (4:8, 16) dominates this section, and extends into the next one. This claim is unique to 1 John in the New Testament, although its ancestry can be traced back through the Fourth Gospel to the message of Jesus himself about the merciful nature of God's reign and the centrality of love for following God's ways. Indeed, *hesed,* faithful covenant love, is one of the fundamental characteristics ascribed to God in the Hebrew Scriptures. Like the closely related assertion that God is light in 1:5 (see the comments there), "God is love" is not a speculative statement about the divine nature, but a claim about God's actions. Love is a personal activity, not an abstract quality. In saying that God *is* love, 1 John means to assert that God *does* love, as verses 9-10 make clear.

Verses 7-10 explore the nature of God's love as the basis for love among God's children. Because God's nature and characteristic activity is to love, our love for one another is the result of our being born of God and knowing God. Moreover, the love that God has always been was revealed in the merciful sending of Christ into the world to give life to human beings. Thus, both God's act in sending the Son and the Son's act in giving up his life define love as the yielding of self-interest for the sake of others—not an attitude or an impulse, not even simply an emotion, but a concrete *kind of action.* It is this love that the author desires of his readers. Along with 3:16-17, this is as much discussion as 1 John ever gives of what it means to love one another. It is left to the reader to discover the implications of love; but the basic direction cannot be doubted.

Verses 9-10 make a strong appeal to Johannine tradition in support of the Christology and the call to love that are the essence of 1 John's message. The idea that God "sent" Jesus pervades the Gospel of John, indeed is a defining feature of its Christology (e.g., John 5:23-24, 36-38; 7:16-18, 28-29; 17:3, 18-25). The sending of the Son is a self-revelation of God (John 1:18; 8:19; 14:7-11); and if God is love, then it is this love in particular that is revealed in Jesus. There is probably a deliberate reference to John 3:16 here as well. Though the world often represents danger and opposition in Johannine thought (see 4:4-6, and the comments on 2:15-17), even in 1 John it can also be the object of God's love. Verse 10 adds two significant points. Love is not something that we initiate, but first comes to us as a gift from God (see also 4:19). Then, using the exact language of 2:2 (see the comments there), "the atoning sacrifice for our sins" makes explicit what is only implied in John 3:16: God not only sent the Son, but sent him to offer up his life for human sins. It is this love that sacrifices its own interests for those of the beloved that reveals the God of love.

Verse 11 begins a new unit by renewing the exhortation to love, using the logic of the imitation of God (see 1:5-7 and especially 2:28–3:10): Those who are born of God should do as God does. (On the verb "ought," see the comments on 2:6.) This exhortation will be supported by the themes enunciated in verse 12, mutual abiding with God (vv. 13-16) and the perfection of God's love (vv. 17-18). In introducing these themes, verse 12 again appeals to Johannine tradition, in the words "no one has ever seen God" (based on Exod 33:19-23; note also 1 John 3:2; 4:20). According to John 1:18, this unseen God was nevertheless made known by the *monogenēs* (the "only" one, an adjective just applied to the Son in v. 9 here; see also John 5:37; 6:46; 14:7-11). The reader expects, then, that verse 12 will also declare how the unseen God is made known, and so it does: God abides in those who love one another, and in this way God's love reaches perfection in them. The God who is love, once revealed in the sending of the only Son, continues to be made known in the love that Christians show one another. The point is underlined by the repetition of "in us": *Christian love is the ongoing revelation of God.*

The perfection of God's love in those who keep the word of God was affirmed in 2:5, and the same basic claim is made here, since the "word" is the love commandment (2:7-11). "His love" probably means God's love for us (subjective genitive) rather than our love for God (objective genitive). But what can it mean to say that God's love is "perfected"? The verb *teleioō* in usages like this means "complete, finish, bring to the goal" (John 4:34; 5:36; 17:4). The thought is not that God's love was ever imperfect, but that it only reaches its intended completion in those who love one another. Acts of Christian love are a necessary part of the process of God's love doing what it is meant to do; divine love is not finished without our love.

This revelation of God in Christian love is further discussed in verses 13-16 and 17-18. The first discussion takes up a theme hinted at in 3:23-24, the unity among the Spirit (v. 13), right Christology (vv. 14-15), and love (v. 16) in assuring Christians of their mutual abiding with God. This theme may be related to the new covenant promise that the people would know God and God would dwell among them (Jer 31:31-34; Ezek 36:27-28; 37:26-28), extended to include both God's presence *within* believers and their presence in God (Malatesta 1978, 306-7). In asserting that Christians abide directly in God and God in them, 1 John also differs from the Fourth Gospel, where Jesus is always the intermediary between them (see further the comments on 2:6 and 3:24).

The discernment formula "by this we know" in verse 13 really covers the entire development in verses 13-16: By all these means believers can be assured of abiding in God and God in them. There is also a *progression* from one criterion to the next. The most recently mentioned criterion was the possession of the Spirit (3:24), and verse 13 simply repeats this. But reference to the Spirit must now take in the discussion in 4:1-6: The presence of *God's* Spirit is certified by the true christological confession that this Spirit enables. Therefore the confession itself follows in verses 14-15: Those who make this confession have the Spirit, and so God abides in them and they in God. The "we" in verse 14 is emphatic. The author and readers who confess this Christology possess the Spirit and abide in God, but by the same token the opponents do not, though they undoubtedly claimed to do so. Moreover, by framing the confession in terms of the *sending* of the Son, the author recalls verses 9-10, which interpret the confession as a recognition of God's love. With another emphatic "we," those who confess the incarnational Christology are now identified as the ones who know and believe this love (v. 16). It is they who can genuinely assert that God is love, and with the repetition of this claim from verse 8 the discussion comes full circle. To abide in love is to abide in God; truly to confess Jesus, the self-revelation of the God who is love, requires loving one another. Thus, the assertion of verse 12 that the unseen God abides in those who love one another is fully demonstrated, using the terms of 3:23-24. All the criteria for mutual indwelling with God—right Christology, the experience of the Spirit, keeping the commandments—have their final criterion in love. The true Spirit inspires and is known by true Christology; but true Christology is only present among believers who love, and so carry out the commandments. Those who desire communion with God must love one another, for by so doing they live out the nature of God. And because God has been revealed in the crucified Jesus, abiding in love does not mean clinging to a warm feeling, but persisting in self-giving *acts* of love.

The relation of the Spirit to christological teaching was noted in the comments on 2:20, 27; 3:24. The Spirit that signals God's mutual indwelling with the Johannine Christians thus also enables their testimony to the sending of the Son (see further 5:6-8). This testimony is to what they have *seen*, another aspect of the way in which the unseen God (v. 12) is revealed. The combination of seeing and testifying recalls the prologues to both 1 John and the Gospel of John (also John 1:34; 3:11, 32; 19:35). "We" may mean the Spirit-guided tradition-bearers whom the author represents, but here it probably also includes the readers, thus once more drawing them onto the author's side.

Jesus is called "Savior of the world" only in verse 14 and John 4:42 in the New Testament. Elsewhere this hellenistic title is used to speak of Jesus as Savior of Christians as a group (e.g., Eph 5:23; 2 Tim 1:10; Titus 3:4-6; 2 Pet 1:1, 11), or of Israel (e.g., Luke 2:11; Acts 13:23); note also 1 Tim 4:10. John 3:17; 12:47 emphasize that God sent Jesus as Savior, not judge, of the world. (Regarding "the world," see the comments above on v. 9, and on 2:2; regarding "sending," see the comments on v. 10.) The confessional formula in verse 15 is comparable to those in 2:22; 4:2-3; 5:1, 5. In the Gospel of John, assertions that Jesus is the Son of God are directed against denials of his divinity (e.g., John 1:34; 3:18; 10:31-36; 11:27; 20:31). In 1 John the point seems to be not the divinity of Jesus but the humanity of the Son of God. The opponents might agree that God sent the Son to save us and give us life; but for the author this confession is not complete if it is not the human Jesus who is this Son sent from God. Therefore the opponents' mission cannot really bring the Savior to the world (see the comments on 4:5).

In verse 16, "we" clearly includes not just the author and his party but the readers as well. This love is literally said to be "in us" or "among us" *(en hēmin)*, the same words as in verse 9. The common translation "for us" is unlikely, since the preposition *en* expresses direction only with verbs of motion or putting. It is not simply that God has this love "toward us"; rather, this love is expressed "in our midst" by the sending of the Son. Moreover, the present tense verb "has," in contrast to the past tenses of verses 9-10, points to the ongoing presence of God's love in the love presently at work "in us," that is, in Christian love for one another. (See further Malatesta 1984.)

The second of the two small special discussions initiated by verse 12 deals with perfected love in relation to confidence at the last judgment (vv. 17-18). "In this" in verse 17 refers forward to the clause "that we may have boldness"; eschatological confidence is thus the substance of perfected love (NRSV, NJB, NAB, CEV). (If it referred backward instead, to v. 16, it would simply reprise v. 12, and confidence would be the *aim* of perfected love; so NIV, REB, but this leaves the last clause of the verse dangling.) The perfection of God's love consists in confidence at the judgment, because perfected love brings with it a likeness to Jesus.

This confidence (or "boldness") thus has the same basis as that in 2:28–3:3. The pronoun *ekeinos* ("he"), as always in 1 John, refers to Jesus and to imitation of him (see the comments on 2:3-6). Likeness to Jesus consists primarily in loving as he did (2:6-11; 3:16); those who love abide in God and God in them, as was and is the case with Jesus (John 10:38; 14:10-11, 20; 17:21-23). Thus, they are "as he is" (not as he *was;* see the comments on 2:8) "in this world" (see 3:3-7). In Johannine realized eschatology, Christians have in effect already transcended the judgment (John 5:24). Living in love is already living the eschatological life of communion with God, the life beyond the judgment (1 John 3:14). In this life of love "there is no fear" (v. 18). Despite the tempting generality of this expression, its meaning is to be sought in its specifically eschatological context. It is fear of the judgment that is expelled by perfect love, the love for one another that brings God's love to its completion. (For the contrast between confidence and fear at the judgment, see Wis 5:1-2; 2 Esdr 7:87, 98.)

The term for punishment *(kolasis)* is a common one in early Christian eschatology (e.g., Matt 25:46). The Greek of verse 18 literally says that fear "has punishment." This is usually translated "has *to do with* punishment," but is more naturally understood as "receives, expects to receive, deserves punishment" (*Herm. Sim.* 9.18.1). What seems to be needed here is something that means the opposite—not "fear receives punishment" but "(the prospect of) punishment causes fear," so that love, which knows that no punishment is coming, has no fear. It may be that the author meant this, and has simply expressed himself obscurely once again. If he really does mean that fear leads to punishment, the point may be that fear shows an awareness of not having imitated Jesus in love, and is thus the precursor (if not exactly the cause) of punishment. It is at any rate clear why "whoever fears has not reached perfection in love." "Perfection in love" means God's love brought to its intended goal in Christian love for one another; and this love eliminates fear of the judgment.

◊ ◊ ◊ ◊

It is not easy to reconcile the claim that God is love with biblical statements about divine wrath, in the New Testament as well as in the Hebrew Scriptures. First John offers only one proof for this claim. God's action in the sending of the Son as expiation for human sins, and Jesus' action in laying down his life, are the demonstration that God is love, and the revelation of the nature of this love as one that gives itself up for the beloved. Against the opponents, 1 John insists that incarnational Christology and an ethic of active love are indispensable and utterly inseparable. The human life and death of Jesus the Son of God are not incidental but essential as the revelation of the love that God is; and precisely this act of self-sacrificing love enables, exemplifies, and evokes Christian love. Anything that contradicts such a love is ruled out for the people who are "of God"—including many actions that profess to be done out of love but really express a desire to dominate and control.

This may be part of the reason why 1 John itself urges and persuades, but asserts no authoritarian claims. Though he addresses the readers as "children," the author never demands their obedience, never threatens or even (in 1 John, at least) gives them orders. Yet it is far from clear that even he fully succeeded in imitating the God who is love. The association of the opponents with "the world" may embody a necessary theological judgment, but it also verges on placing them beyond the pale of Christian love (see the comments on 5:1, 16). The instructions to refuse hospitality in 2 John 10-11 put that exclusion into practice. This struggle between the inclusive vision of God as love and the restrictive demand for control has been repeated all too often in Christian history.

The experience of God is not purely individual but communal in 1 John, since it can be validated only by love for one another. Mutual indwelling with God is an "interior" phenomenon, but two of the three criteria for discerning it in 4:13-16 are external activities: christological confession and love. Indeed, it has been suggested that by claiming that God is love, 1 John declares it *impossible* to know God except in loving other people (Wengst 1976, 71-73; Miranda 1977, 137-48). This may be somewhat overstated, but it is fundamental to Johannine theology that genuine knowledge of God, true abiding in God, is found only in Jesus, who carries out God's works of love, and in the loving actions of those who believe in him. On the other hand, 1 John also asserts that the initiative in love belongs to God, so that Christian love is the *result* of relationship to God, not its cause (Malatesta 1984, 308-9, though Malatesta may exaggerate in the opposite direction). This seems to raise a question of priority: Does our knowledge of the God who is love cause us to love one another, or is it our love for one another that allows us to know God? But the alternative is a false one in 1 John's terms, which do not really allow such a logic of sequence. God is revealed to us as love in Jesus the Christ, but we cannot accept or understand this revelation without taking upon ourselves the life of love for one another. We love one another because we have known God in Jesus Christ; yet without love we do not truly know this God at all.

## LOVING GOD (4:19–5:5)

Given the clear way in which 4:18 rounds off the preceding section, and the parallel expressions in 4:7, 11, and 19, a new section probably begins at 4:19, though most commentators delay it until 5:1. The end of the section is a bit harder to locate. Most English versions place a break after 5:5. There would also be some merit in placing one after 5:4 (NJB; Marshall 1978; Schnackenburg 1992), or even after 5:4a (Brown 1982). That would pull apart the tight inclusion formed by the repetition of "who believes that Jesus is" in 5:1 and 5:5, however. This inclusion marks off a distinct unit emphasizing Christology, although 5:1 is also tightly connected to 4:21. Thus it seems best to regard 4:19–5:5 as a section, with 4:19-21 and 5:1-5 as its subunits.

First John 4:7-18 had spoken of the connection between God's love for believers and their love for one another. Here, 4:19 speaks simply of their love, without specifying its object, and then 4:20 introduces the relation between their love for *God* and that for their brothers and sisters. Thus, 4:19 makes a transition from love for one another to love for God. The further discussion in 4:21 then leads into 5:1-3: the logic of 4:21 is explained in 5:1, and 5:2-3 relates love for God's children to love for God in terms of the commandments. But 5:1 also introduces the subject of Christology, which is then taken up in 5:4-5, in relation to "conquering the world." Thus introduced, true christological faith will become the sole theme in 5:6-12. (See the comments below for the details of these transitions.)

The movement from 4:19 to 5:5, from love to Christology, is linguistically (if not logically) seamless; without noticing how, we simply find ourselves in the midst of an entirely different topic at the end of the section from the one at the beginning. The indissoluble unity between Christology and love was already made clear in 3:23; and now, after the discussions of Christology in 4:1-6 and love in 4:7-18, the strange continuity of 4:19–5:5 implies it once again. To be born of God is defined by these two things (4:7; 5:1). Their unity is the bedrock of our author's theology, and for all his sometimes irritating clumsiness and obscurity, here at least he has enacted the content of his message rather profoundly in its form.

◊ ◊ ◊ ◊

First John 4:19 repeats in the simplest possible way the thought of 4:7, 11. (See also 4:10 on the priority of God's love.) Despite its simplicity, however, the verse raises two questions. First, the verb *agapōmen* can be either indicative ("we love") or subjunctive ("let us love"). Most English translations and commentators choose the former, on the basis of the context and the presence of the emphatic pronoun "we." But the pronoun simply contrasts with the equally emphatic "he," and this balance is just as effective with a subjunctive as with an indicative. As for the context, the whole tone of 1 John, especially the immediately preceding passages, is of an *exhortation* to love. In the parallel 4:7, 11 we find, respectively, the same verb in a clearly subjunctive use, and the exhortation "we also *ought* to love." The only difference here is the lack of an expressed object, which leads to the second question. The best manuscripts have no direct object for *agapōmen*. Comparison with 4:7, 11 suggests that "one another" might be the implied object of "love"; but the discussion of loving God in 4:20–5:3 suggests that the implied object should be "God." In fact, the author probably deliberately left the object unspecified, so that verse 19 could function as a transition from the theme of love for one another in 4:7-18 to that of love for God in 4:20–5:5. In the end, the best translation is probably, "Let us love, because he first loved us."

The new development that begins in 4:20 opens with strong echoes of 1:5–2:11. The form of the construction "if anyone says" (NRSV: "those who say") resembles the "boasts" in 1:6, 8, 10, while the content, "I love God," recalls those in 2:4, 6, 9. The reference to lying is also reminiscent of 1:6; 2:4; in both places, part of the issue is inconsistency between words and deeds. Love for God, not a prominent topic previously in 1 John, was apparently the subject in 2:5, and love and hatred for brothers and sisters was the theme of 2:9-11. Thus, as it draws near its end 1 John presents a striking inclusion with its beginning. This suggests that 4:20, like 1:5–2:11, is aimed specifically at the opponents, who claimed to love God but did not love their sisters and brothers in the Johannine community. (The NRSV use of inclusive plurals heightens this sense of a communal controversy.) As elsewhere in 1 John, the opponents' lack of love (which, in the author's dualism, is equivalent to hatred) must have been demonstrated by concrete actions, such as their leaving the community and their neglect of material help for the poor (2:19; 3:15-17).

The form of 4:20b follows the well-known ancient logical pattern of argument from the lesser to the greater (a minori ad maius; Hebrew qal wāḥōmer). The sentence is not a syllogism, however, but parenesis, and the point is not that loving people is an easier first step toward the more difficult level of loving God. Rather, love for people provides a test that is more easily verified. The underlying basis, moreover, is 4:12: The unseen God is revealed in love for one another (see the comments there); therefore, those who do not practice love cannot love this God, who remains unknown to them (3:6; 4:8).

First John 4:21 takes up again the idea of the commandment (2:7-11; 3:23-24), but also introduces something new. No commandment in precisely this form is found in John or 1 John. There is, of course, the Johannine tradition that those who love Jesus keep his commandments, and that his commandment is to love one another (John 13:34; 14:15, 21-24; 15:10, 12, 17). It could well be that this tradition has simply been transferred from Jesus to God here, a pattern typical of 1 John (see the introduction). On the other hand, this commandment is remarkably similar to Jesus' teaching about the two primary commandments according to Mark 12:28-34 (see the comments on 3:23). It is possible that this, rather than the specifically Johannine traditions, was in the author's mind, since he also has a habit of introducing non-Johannine materials. (Despite REB, however, in 1 John the giver of the love commandment is always God, not Jesus.)

The full sense of this commandment is only brought out in 5:1-3, however, and there the Johannine logic prevails. In this logic, to love God is to obey God's commandments, one of which is the commandment of mutual love. The other commandment is to believe in Jesus, which brings birth from God (John 1:12-13). Since those who love the parent will naturally love the child as well, whoever loves God must love God's other children, that is, their brothers and sisters who likewise believe in Jesus.

This would be enough to clarify 4:21. The definition of God's children in terms of Johannine Christology also serves to introduce the christological discussion of chapter 5, however. (Note that elsewhere in 1 John, birth from God is signaled by loving actions rather than Christology; see 2:29; 3:9-10; 4:7; 5:18, with the comments.) As noted above, the confession of Jesus in 5:1 forms an inclusion with 5:5. A comparison with John 20:31 shows that the predicates "Christ" and "Son of God" are parts of a single whole. (Note also "his Son Jesus Christ" in 1 John 1:3; 3:23; 5:20, and the confessional formulas in 2:22-23; 4:2-3, 15.) The full title thus forms the structural bracket for this unit. It also defines the Christology that the author promotes, against his opponents, in the following discussion. John 20:31 itself is an interpretive key, remaining constantly in the background through the rest of 1 John.

In supporting his position by an appeal to Johannine tradition, combining John 1:12-13 with 20:31 and the love commandment, the author gives the tradition new and potentially disturbing implications. As in 4:15, the issue is no longer the divinity of Jesus but the humanity of the Son of God. Being a child of God comes from christological faith, but that faith must be in the human Jesus as the Christ, the Son of God. First John 4:20-21 had not placed any restriction on love for brothers and sisters. This definition of birth from God, however, excludes the opponents with their different Christology; if its logic were pressed to the limit it would not recognize them as sisters and brothers who are to be loved. As 2 John shows, the epistles do at least come near such an exclusion, and it is possible that the author and the opponents each (for rather different reasons) claimed that the other need not be an object of love (Brown 1982, 84-86, 565-67). Here, though, the immediate point at issue is the opponents' failure to love and to believe, not whether they themselves should be loved.

First John 5:2 contains the last of the discernment formulas that occur throughout 1 John (see the comments on 2:3), and it presents a difficult exegetical problem. Generally, "in this" (NRSV: "by this") in these formulas refers to something that follows (the only exceptions are 2:5; 3:19). If it does so here, however, the verse seems to say the exact opposite of what one would expect. Instead of saying that love for God must be verified by love for one another (as in 4:20–5:1; cf. 2:3-5; 3:17; 4:8, 12, 16), it says that love for God's children must be verified by love for God. The problem would be relieved if "in this" referred backward, so that one could translate, "In this [i.e., the statement of 5:1b] we know that we love God's children whenever we love God and do his commandments" (NAB, REB; Dodd 1946, 125; Marshall 1978, 227-28). This seems an unlikely way of construing "when(ever)" *(hotan),* however, so that "in this" probably must refer forward, as usual.

The surprising statement that love for God's children is to be verified by love for God must be interpreted in terms of its literary function and the conflict with the opponents. First John 5:1-5, though tightly knit in itself, is transitional, a "hinge" unit (see the literary analysis of this section). It is based on 4:21 (love), but introduces 5:6-12 (Christology). The author is shifting from criticizing the opponents' lack of love back to criticizing their Christology, and the shift takes place in 5:2-3. The "commandments" in verse 2 cannot be restricted to the love commandment without creating a tautology (we know that we love God's children when we keep God's commandment to love them). Yet the commandments in verse 3 cannot be restricted to Christology, or 5:3-5 also becomes tautological (those who have the right Christology find it easy to have the right Christology). Both commandments are in view in both verses; but the emphasis is shifting from love to belief.

This suggests a new aspect of the unity of mutual love and right Christology. Love involves commitment and faithfulness. Part of Christians' faithfulness to other Christians is their faithfulness to the God whose children they all are (Westcott 1892, 177-78), that is, their obedience to God's commandments, *including the commandment of right Christology* (von Wahlde 1990, 66). Moreover, since this God was revealed as love in the incarnation (4:8-10, 14-16), faithfulness to love requires faithfulness to incarnational Christology. The same thought is expressed in 2 John 6. It is not well prepared for here, but it evidently *is* the thought, and it provides the necessary transition from love to Christology.

The idea that God's commandments are not burdensome has roots in Deut 30:11-14 (see also Matt 11:28-30). Here, however, it is specifically victory over the world through belief in Jesus that makes keeping the commandments easy (cf. Rom 8:1-14). This conquest was alluded to in 4:4-5, where the world is associated with the opponents, and already hinted at in 2:12-17, where the conquest of the evil one is followed by an injunction against loving the world. According to 5:18-19, the evil one cannot cause the one born of God to sin, though the world lies in his power. The thought here is much the same: The world resists God's commandments, but those who conquer the world can keep the commandments. This whole complex of ideas is derived from John 16:33, where Jesus conquers the world, and from the Johannine conception of the devil as the "ruler of this world" (John 12:31; 14:30; 16:11; note also 17:15). Jesus conquers the world and its ruler as Son of God, and those who hold the right christological belief share in his victory, since they also are God's children (the same pattern as in 5:1; see also 3:8).

Several linguistic details give nuance to 5:4. The neuter "whatever is born of God" (rather than "whoever") is surprising. It may be intended to refer to children of God in the aggregate (cf. the neuters referring to groups of people in John 3:6; 6:37, 39; 17:2, 7, 24). The use of the aorist participle *nikēsasa* ("that has conquered"; NRSV: "that conquers") in 5:4*b* may suggest that the victory of faith is rooted in some moment of the past, either the believers' conversion or Jesus' own victory. The noun "faith" itself *(pistis)* is an example of 1 John's use of non-Johannine Christian language. Though common elsewhere in the New Testament, it is found only here in the Gospel and epistles of John, which otherwise use forms of the verb "to believe" *(pisteuō)*. As 5:5 makes clear, this is not faith in the general sense of trust in God, but the specific christological faith that is part of the dispute with the opponents. "Faith" thus seems to be edging toward the sense "the faith," that is, the Christian religion (Gal 1:23; 1 Tim 4:1, 6; Jude 3). Yet, despite the almost credal formulations in 5:1, 5, that transition has not yet quite been made. Faith still means *believing*, the act of belief rather than its object.

The logic of this section may have been fairly impressive to its original readers, imbued as they were with Johannine patterns of thought. We are more likely to find it either forced or difficult to follow, especially in 5:1-3. The overall topical movement of the section from love to incarnational faith, enacting the integral unity between the two, may work more powerfully on modern readers. The authentic response to God's love is our love, for God and for one another. Indeed, loving God means loving God's children. For 1 John, however, this is not possible without also acknowledging what God has done in all its fullness: the sending of the Christ, the Son of God, who is the human Jesus. For it is only in him that the love of God is revealed, and through faith in this revelation that the children of God come to birth. All this love is one love; and love and belief twine inseparably around each other, and work indivisibly within each other.

## TESTIMONY TO JESUS THE SON OF GOD (5:6-12)

The christological theme introduced in the preceding section is now developed further. As in 5:1-5, the title "Christ" is used first (v. 6), then "Son" (vv. 9-12). The theme of testimony dominates the section, dividing it along the same lines: the testimony of the Spirit, the water, and the blood occupies verses 6-8, and the testimony of God verses 9-12. Many commentators include the transitional 5:13 with these verses (see the comments on 5:13-21). Testimony and the connection between Jesus and eternal life in verses 11-12 create an inclusion between the ending of 1 John and its prologue (1:2).

◊ ◊ ◊ ◊

We must first note briefly the question of the original text of 5:6-8. Many manuscripts of the Latin Vulgate translation, and a small number of very late Greek manuscripts, have a lengthy addition at the end of verse 7: "three that testify *in heaven, the Father, the Word, and the Holy Spirit, and these three are one. And there are three that testify on earth,* the Spirit. . . . " Textual critics agree that this so-called Comma Johanneum arose in Latin, perhaps in the fourth century, and was later imported into a few Greek manuscripts. (Brown 1982, 775-87, lays out the evidence in detail.) Unfortunately, the added words were incorporated into the Greek text commonly printed from the sixteenth century until the rise of modern critical editions (the "Textus Receptus"), and so were also included in the KJV. They have no claim to an authentic place in the text of 1 John, and are rightly omitted by contemporary English translations.

This section presents an immediate problem in the assertion that Jesus Christ "came by water and blood," and "not with the water only." How did Jesus Christ come "by" or "with" these things? Is the change of prepositions significant? Why the emphatic denial of "water only"? Beyond this, how do these things "testify," and how is their testimony related to that of the Spirit? Presumably the first readers, familiar with the controversy that lay behind these statements, understood them well enough. We must work with the few clues available.

As to the prepositions, though the Greek has first *dia,* literally "through," and then *en,* literally "in," the change does not in fact seem to affect the meaning. The concern for definition, the reference to Jesus' "coming," and the role of the Spirit are reminiscent of 4:2, implying that 5:6 is also a confessional formula. Other features of verses 6-8 recall passages in the Gospel of John. The reference to water and blood is strongly reminiscent of John 19:34-35; the themes of water, Spirit, and testimony are reminiscent of 1:32-34. Both passages must be kept in mind in the following discussion. Testimony to Jesus, moreover, is a central theme of the Fourth Gospel (John 1:7-8, 15, 32-34; 3:11, 32-33; 5:31-47; 8:17-18; 15:26-27; 19:34-35; 21:24).

"Water and blood" is often thought to refer to the Christian sacraments of baptism and eucharist, at least in verses 7-8 (e.g., Houlden 1973, 128-32; Brown 1982, 582-85; Schnackenburg 1992, 236-37; Strecker 1996, 182-86). This is unlikely, since "blood" alone is never used to refer to the eucharist. Yet in a Christian context "water" must surely refer in some way to baptism; given the resemblance to the testimony of John the Baptist in John 1:32-34, the most likely reference is to *Jesus'* baptism. The opponents may have held that the divine, spiritual Christ or Son of God descended or began to be revealed (John 1:31) at that moment (so in various ways Marshall 1978, 232; Brown 1982, 578, 595-96; Schnackenburg 1992, 232-33; Wengst 1976, 18-22). Thus, the "water only" had significance for them as a revelation of divine Spirit. (Note also the connection of water and Spirit in John 3:5; 7:37-39; and see the introduction.)

Whatever the opponents' precise point with regard to "water only," by insisting on *blood* as well as water, the author probably means that Jesus' death as well as his baptism brought revelation and salvation (see 1:7; 2:2; 4:9-10, and the comments there). The opponents, emphasizing the superiority of the spiritual over the material, did not see saving significance in Jesus' violent death; they may even have read John 19:30 as meaning that the divine Spirit left Jesus at the crucifixion. The author insists that Jesus Christ came—came to make God known—in both water and blood, that he accomplished both revelation and salvation not simply through a glorious epiphany of Spirit but in the sacrifice of his own life.

The "testimony" of water and blood must mean something like this. What is the testimony of the Spirit, then? The association of the Spirit with truth is constant in the Johannine writings (2:27; 4:6; John 4:23-24; 14:17; 16:13), and in John 15:26 the Spirit of truth testifies to Jesus. Now, John 19:34-35 insists that the testimony *to* the blood and water at Jesus' crucifixion is "true." First John 5:6 seems to be appealing to this tradition, perhaps even to this text. The author wants to identify the testimony to the blood and water in John 19:34-35 as that of the Spirit, because the Spirit is truth and the testimony is said to be true. The Spirit of truth testifies to everything that is true about Jesus Christ—including his blood, his death.

The community likely understood the Johannine tradition as a whole, including 19:34, as the testimony of the Spirit (John 15:26-27; see also 14:26; 16:12-15). The opponents may have seen the revelation to John the Baptist as a testimony of the Spirit to the coming of the Son "in the water" (see John 1:32-34). They certainly claimed that the Spirit inspired and legitimated their own teaching (4:1-3). Our author, by contrast, asserts that the Spirit actually testifies to the human Jesus and to his death, that is, to incarnational Christology. In this way the Spirit testifies to the water and the blood, and thereby validates them so that they also testify alongside the Spirit. Thus there are three witnesses (perhaps with Deut 19:15 in mind). These three "agree," literally, "are into [or toward] the one [thing]" *(eis to hen eisin)*. One might translate this unusual expression "the three are at one," or "attest to the one thing" (NJB: "coincide"). That one thing is undoubtedly the true incarnation of Jesus Christ, the fact of his death and its significance for salvation.

The contrast between human and divine testimony in verse 9 raises the question of what each of them is. "Human testimony" might, of course, not refer to any specific testimony, but simply contrast in general with the testimony of God. If something precise is meant, it is probably not the testimony of the Johannine tradition, which the preceding verses identify as the testimony of the Spirit. Rather, we should look to John 5:31-38, where the human testimony of John the Baptist is contrasted with the greater testimony of God. (Note also John 3:31-33, which contrasts the Baptist's earthly words with the heavenly ones of Jesus.) As suggested above, the opponents may have appealed to the testimony of John the Baptist as proving that Jesus' baptism was the moment when the divine Son was revealed. The author would be subtly criticizing them here by pointing out that while "we" do accept the Baptist's testimony, it is not the highest testimony, and that Jesus himself did not accept it.

The testimony of God is even harder to identify. It could, of course, simply be identical with the testimony of the Spirit (and the water and the blood) previously discussed. Yet "this" in the kind of formula used in verse 9 generally points forward, not backward (so 5:4, 6, 11, 14; also 2:22, 25; 3:11, 23; 2 John 6). Moreover, "this is the testimony" is repeated in verse 11, where the testimony is explicitly identified. This repetition of the formula suggests that verse 10 is a parenthesis, so that the identification of God's testimony, begun in verse 9, is not really given until verse 11. This is confirmed by the further repetition of "has testified concerning his Son" at the end of verse 10, which produces a kind of chiasm. (Despite the NRSV, the Greek at the ends of vv. 9 and 10 is identical.)

The question is complicated by the presence of the ambiguous particle *hoti* twice in verse 9*b*. (See the comments on 3:19-20. The NIV apparently follows an inferior group of manuscripts that replace the second *hoti* with a relative pronoun.) The first *hoti* clearly means "because" or "for"; the problem is the second one. If it is taken as a neuter relative (*ho ti*, "that which") with the antecedent unexpressed, the result is a mere tautology: "for this is the testimony of God: *that which* he has testified concerning his Son" (so apparently REB). It could also be epexegetical or declarative, explaining what God's testimony is or introducing its content as an indirect quotation: "for this is the testimony of God, *that* he has testified concerning his Son." Though this interpretation is widely adopted, it seems a worse tautology yet. It can hardly be meant to emphasize that God is the giver of the testimony, and the form given it by the NRSV leaves the referent of "this" hopelessly unclear. But the second *hoti* could also mean "for," like the first, in which case the content of the testimony is simply not given in this verse: "for this is the testimony of God—*for* he has testified concerning his Son." On the whole, this explanation, clumsy as it sounds, is the least improbable. It also agrees with the interpretation suggested above. The testimony is not identified until verse 11;

verses 9d-10, beginning and ending with "(for) he has testified concerning his Son," build up the reader's suspense about what the testimony is.

Verse 10 seems to allude to John 3 (perhaps because of the prominence of John the Baptist in that context). The structure "those who believe in . . . those who do not believe . . . for they have not believed in" (AT) is reminiscent of John 3:18, though the content is different. "Those who do not believe in God have made him a liar" is essentially a negative form of John 3:33. Moreover, verse 12 seems to be a reformulation of John 3:36. The author thus continues to appeal to traditions and texts that were held in common by all Johannine Christians, including the opponents. The same is true of the affirmation in verse 11 that God has given us eternal life (closer to classic Johannine realized eschatology than 2:25 is). The opponents might even have acknowledged that this life is in the Son, so that those and only those who have the Son have life (on "having the Son," see the comments on 2:23). Indeed, given John 1:3-4; 3:16, 36; 5:26; 11:25; 14:6, they could hardly have done otherwise. What they evidently denied was that this life-giving Son of God was identical with the human Jesus.

The allusion to John 20:31 introduced in 5:1, 5 remains a strong factor here: It is faith in *Jesus* the Son of God that gives eternal life, and accordingly it is those who accept 1 John's incarnational Christology who have this life. In the author's view, since Jesus is the Son of God in whom eternal life has been given, indeed *is* eternal life incarnate (1:2), life itself is God's own testimony to Jesus' identity. By denying this identity, the opponents rejected God's testimony and so made God a liar—an enormity in a tradition wherein the reality of God was called "truth" (see also 1:10). Since eternal life is God's testimony, it must be this life that the believer has as the testimony within (v. 10). The NRSV translation "in their hearts" (similarly NIV) is somewhat misleading. The Greek says simply "in himself," which does not necessarily mean an "inner witness" of the Spirit or the like. To possess God's gift of eternal life through faith in the Son is to possess God's testimony to the Son. The testimony within the believer is thus not a subjective experience, but a theological "fact."

The somewhat confusing arrangement of verses 9-12 may obscure what was for the author a reasonably simple point. Backed by a series of traditions found in the Gospel of John, all governed by John 20:31, the author asserts that God has testified to incarnational Christology, with its claim that the Son of God has come in the human Jesus. This testimony consists in the eternal life that God has given to those who believe this christological claim. Believers have this life, and therefore possess this testimony. Those who do not so believe (i.e., the opponents) risk losing both the truth of God and the eternal life that is central to the Johannine understanding of salvation.

◊ ◊ ◊ ◊

As elsewhere in 1 John, we find in this section a number of allusions to Johannine traditions, perhaps even to texts of the Fourth Gospel; we also find an appeal to the testimony of the Spirit. This reminds us that the controversy to which 1 John was responding was in part a controversy over the meaning of the community's Johannine heritage. Which traditions, those about the coming of the Son of God in glory or those about the human life and death of Jesus, should control the community's understanding of Christ? Where was the ongoing activity of the Spirit to be seen in the community?

For 1 John, the testimony of the Spirit takes place not only in new teaching but in the tradition handed down, including the tradition about Jesus' physical death (Schnackenburg 1971, 142-44; Klauck 1989, 212-14). Teaching that contradicts this tradition cannot be from the Spirit. The incarnational tradition, being the testimony of the Spirit, thus provides a means of evaluating other claims to the Spirit. This may be a first step toward the canonization of the Johannine tradition, and specifically of its written form, the Gospel of John. (See the concluding comments on 2:18-27.) Yet the interpretation of this tradition is itself at issue. For 1 John, the key to understanding the tradition correctly is the element of incarnational Christology within it. It is in this sense that one might speak of a *regula fidei,* a rule of faith, in 1 John (Wengst 1976, 64-65), that is, a doctrinal conception used as a criterion for evaluating beliefs and even interpretations of the authoritative tradition. There can be no doubt that this involves a circular argument, as incarnational Christology is used to interpret the tradition, which is then claimed as confirmation of incarnational Christology. Such circularity may be inevitable in any group that appeals to traditions from the past to decide current disputes, but the typical patterns of Johannine language and thought only exacerbate it.

Nevertheless, 1 John does seem to be correct in its claim that the Incarnation, the revelation of God in the human person of Jesus, including his crucifixion, is central and indispensable to the Gospel of John. John may say that Jesus' death is his "lifting up," his "glorification" (3:14; 8:28; 12:23, 32-33; 13:31-33; 17:1, 5), but in these very passages it is clear that Jesus' mission of making God known is carried out in his death, and indeed precisely in the manner of it as crucifixion. At the moment of his death, Jesus cries out that his task has been accomplished (John 19:30). First John is right to insist that it is in his death—his bloody death—that the Johannine Jesus carries out his Father's commandment (John 10:17-18; 14:30-31) and so accomplishes both salvation and revelation. The victorious God of eternal life is revealed, and proffers this life, in the violent death of a human victim of oppression. The Johannine tradition offers this paradox, and not a spiritualized resolution of it, as the gospel message, and, however obscure his wording may sometimes be, our author has grasped this truth with a grip of iron.

## FINAL REFLECTIONS (5:13-21)

First John 5:13 so closely resembles John 20:31, the original ending of the Fourth Gospel, that it seems obviously meant to conclude 1 John as a whole. However, the themes of John 20:31 (eternal life, belief, the Son of God) already stood in the background of 1 John 5:1-12, so that verse 13 climaxes its immediate context as well. Moreover, the ideas of the Son and eternal life form an inclusion with 5:20, confirming that verse 13 also begins the closing section. It is, in fact, the final "hinge" verse, linking what precedes and follows it.

Verses 14-21 can hardly be said to draw the text to an orderly close. They are not so much conclusion as epilogue, which may partly account for their disjointedness. Even "epilogue" may be too formal a term. They are an assemblage of reflections on various themes from 1 John: prayer; sin; the world and the evil one; God, the Son, and eternal life. Surprisingly, the two main themes, love and right Christology, show up only in muted and indistinct forms. Differences from the rest of 1 John, and the fact that verse 13 seems to be a conclusion, have led some to suggest that verses 14-21 come from a later redactor (Bultmann 1967b, 383-88; Bultmann 1973, 2; Wengst 1978, 21). But the supposed differences are overdrawn, and the reason for such a redaction, and particularly for verse 21, is left very unclear (Nauck 1957, 134-46; Brown 1982, 632; Strecker 1996, 199-200). Difficult as they are, one must still interpret these verses as the conclusion intended by the author of 1 John. Indeed, "his Son Jesus Christ" and "eternal life" in verse 20 form an inclusion with 1:1-3, and thus round off the entire text.

As for internal structure, prayer connects verses 14-15 to verses 16-17, and sin connects the latter to verse 18. Verses 18-21 have a structure of their own, consisting of three statements of what "we know" (picking up from v. 15, and indeed v. 13). All three involve the contrast between the children of God and the forces of evil arrayed against them, though this is not as obvious in verses 20-21 as elsewhere (see the comments).

◊ ◊ ◊ ◊

Verse 13 states the author's purpose in writing, adding to the statements in 1:4; 2:1. Previously he has assured the readers of his confidence that they know the truth (2:21; see also 2:13-14), and "we know" in 5:18-21 manifestly includes them. It is a bit surprising, then, to read here that his purpose is to let them know that they have eternal life. The opponents may have begun to shake the readers' confidence in their salvation, and therefore one purpose for writing 1 John was to undergird that confidence. It is belief in the traditional Johannine Christology of incarnation, not the novelties of the opponents, that brings eternal life. "Who believe in the name of the Son of God" is in an emphatic position at the end of the sentence in Greek, and strongly echoes not only John 20:31 but John 1:12 as well, grounding the assurance in Johannine tradition. (On the "name" of Jesus, see the comments on 2:12; 3:23.) The *assumption* that the readers share the author's Christology also serves to draw them once again onto his side of the dispute.

This sense of assurance apparently leads to the topic of confident prayer in verse 14: The basis of the readers' confidence is their faith. A similar point was made in 3:21-23 (see the comments there); it is clear from that passage that "in him" refers to God, not Jesus. Asking according to God's will appears to be a rather commonplace hedge on the answering of prayer: Requests will be granted if they are in accord with the divine will. A deeper sense of submission to God's will is possible, however, in the sense of keeping the commandments, as in 3:22. Of course, for 1 John, the divine will is that of the God who is *love*.

The answering of prayer is then given a specific focus, the forgiveness of sin (vv. 16-17). As in 1:5–2:2, it is assumed that Christians can sin, and that effective intercession is available. Here, however, it is not Jesus but other Christians who intercede (cf. the lifesaving intercessions of Abraham [Gen 18:23-33; 20:7] and Moses [Exod 32:9-14], and see also John 20:23). This prayer can be made by "anyone" (*tis;* the NRSV's "you" underscores the gender-inclusiveness). Confession is not mentioned, though perhaps it is presupposed (see the comments on 1:9). It may be the Christian rather than God who will "give life," since the Greek has simply "he/she will pray and he/she will give life" (cf. Jas 5:14-20). On the other hand, abrupt changes of subject occur elsewhere in 1 John (see the comments on 2:3-6 and 2:28–3:1), and in the Johannine writings God or Jesus is always the giver of life (5:11; John 5:21; 6:33, 63; 10:28; 17:2). In either case, what is meant is the *restoration* of life to those who have sinned.

It is the impossibility of restoring life in some cases that creates the "sin that leads to death" (NIV; NRSV: "sin that is mortal"). But what exactly is this sin? (For surveys of the possibilities, see Scholer 1975, 233-38; Brown 1982, 613-19.) Nothing here suggests a ranking of sins, some naturally worse than others (note v. 17*a*), or the unforgivable blasphemy against the Holy Spirit mentioned in Mark 3:28-30. A number of texts in the Hebrew Scriptures place some sins beyond atonement or prayer (e.g., Num 15:27-31; 1 Sam 2:22-25; Isa 22:12-14; Jer 7:16-20; 14:7-12; see also 1QS 8:20–9:2). Such sins tend to involve the worship of other gods, or the deliberate rejection of God or God's ways. The latter is the issue in Heb 6:4-8; 10:26-30. In the Johannine tradition, John 8:21-24; 9:39-41 associate inescapable sin with the rejection of Jesus as the one sent by God. First John has just said that life is given in Jesus (1 John 5:11-13). Thus, the deadly sin may be the opponents' christological denial, which in its way is also a rejection of God. There is another factor as well, however. The only other mention of death in 1 John is at 3:14-15, where failure to love one's brother or sister leaves one abiding in death rather than life (see the comments there). This failure is thus also part of the "sin that leads to death." It includes breaking fellowship with the community, in which alone life is to be found (Whitacre 1982, 137). First John 3:14 alludes to John 5:24, which says that the passage from death to life results from a believing response to Jesus. Thus, the "sin that leads to death" is probably lack of christological faith and lack of love taken together, since precisely this lack cuts one off from eternal life (Scholer 1975, 240-41; Grayston 1984, 144).

These, of course, are the sins being committed by the opponents, who are thereby placed on the wrong side of the Johannine dualism again. Does verse 16 suggest that sisters and brothers in the community may commit this sin? Apparently so (despite Scholer 1975); otherwise the author would not have to specify that the sin to be prayed for is *not* a sin that leads to death. There is thus an implicit warning here against going over to the opponents. The readers, though not explicitly forbidden to pray about this sin, are certainly discouraged from doing so. We might expect that the forgiveness of the opponents' deadly sin and their restoration to fellowship with the community would be the very thing for which the author would most encourage prayer (cf. Ign. *Smyrn.* 4.1). Instead, this verse presents a particularly unhappy example of the restriction of love to "one another." First John 1:7 has a more generous understanding of cleansing from sin in Jesus; yet it too focuses on distinction from the opponents.

There are wrongdoings that do not cut one off from life so drastically, and apparently any Christian may commit these; but they are sin all the same. This leads to perhaps the most difficult contradiction in 1 John. Already 2:28–3:10 seemed to disallow exactly what 1:5–2:2 presupposed, that Christians could sin (see the comments on those passages). As we have seen, verses 16-17 echo 1:5–2:2; but verse 18a is virtually an exact repetition of 3:9a. The author thus draws together the whole thematic involving sin here, and thereby produces an inconsistency of which he cannot possibly have been unaware. There is no indication of any difference between verses 16-17 and verse 18 in the meaning of "sin"; the same tense of the same verb is used in both. Thus verse 18 cannot be taken to refer to the "sin that leads to death," as if only outsiders (including the opponents), but not those born of God, could commit it (Scholer 1975, 244-46; Whitacre 1982, 137-38; Vitrano 1987).

As before, the difficulty may be addressed, if not overcome, by keeping in mind the author's concerns. In 1:5–2:2; 2:28–3:10, these included identifying the true children of God, promoting sinlessness in practice and not just in principle, and keeping the readers from sinning while assuring them that if they do sin all is not lost. All of these aims are present here. The way in which they are pursued may be considered nonlogical, "affective"; the result, unfortunately, is to seem simply illogical. The readers are encouraged to be confident that freedom from sin is part of their birthright as children of God. Yet if they do find sin in their midst, they must still stand by the sinner—so long as it is not the deadly sin of deliberately abandoning mutual love and true belief.

The final verses of 1 John contain three statements of things that "we know," important affirmations that the author hopes will strengthen the readers' resistance to the opponents. All three contrast the children of God with the evil one. The dualism that pervades 1 John thus has its strongest expression here at the very end.

Verse 18, however disconcerting its juxtaposition with verses 16-17, does emphasize assurance. It is not quite clear, though, who protects the children of God from sinning. The Greek reads literally, "We know that everyone who has been born of God does not sin, but the one who was born of God protects." (NRSV uses the inclusive plural "those/them" for the Greek masculine singular.) There are two problems: Is the one who *has been* born of God (perfect tense) the same as the one who *was* born of God (aorist tense); and what pronoun is the object of "protects"? A majority of manuscripts reads "himself," but the better manuscripts read "him." The reading "himself" implies that the two persons "born of God" are the same, namely the Christian, who is thus self-protected. "Him" implies that the first is the Christian and the second probably Christ, by whom the Christian is protected.

Raymond E. Brown (1982, 620-22) accepts the former interpretation, pointing out that in Johannine writings it is never said that Jesus was "born (or begotten) of God," while such statements are made about Christians (John 1:13; 3:3-8; 1 John 2:29; 3:9; 4:7; 5:1, 4). However, it is likewise never said in Johannine writings that Christians protect themselves; even in 1 John 2:13-14, believers conquer the evil one through the word of God abiding in them. In John 17:11-15 it is God and Jesus who protect Christians from the evil one; and according to 1 John 3:5, 8, the Son of God came precisely to do away with sin and undo the works of the devil. Likewise, the assurances in verses 19-20 here are based on the saving actions of God and of Jesus, not on the self-defense of the believer. For the author to say, this once, that Jesus "was born of God" simply recalls the relationship of solidarity and imitation between Christians and Christ that has been so important throughout 1 John (see especially 2:28–3:10). On the whole, then, it seems more likely that the children of God are protected from sinning by the Son of God.

The elements of protection and danger are balanced in verse 19. The readers, with the author, are identified as those who are "of God" (the NRSV's "children" is not in the Greek), who are guarded from the evil one; yet the world at large is controlled by him. This is one of the most strongly dualistic statements of hostility to the world in the New Testment (see also John 12:31; 14:30; 16:11; 2 Cor 4:4; Eph 2:2; Rev 12:9). Gnostic texts sometimes make similar statements (e.g., *Corp. Herm.* 6.4); the Qumran scrolls also provide examples (1QS 3:18–4:1). In 1 John itself we may compare 2:15-17 (see the comments there); 5:4-5. In 4:4-6 the author identified the opponents with the world, and that surely remains part of the point here. Since they belong to the world, they are not from God; and therefore they, like their teaching (4:1-6) and their deeds (3:10, 12), are from the devil. This means that they are part of what endangers the community, but also that their defeat is assured (2:12-14, 17).

The full reference to God's "Son Jesus Christ" in verse 20 recalls the christological affirmations earlier in chapter 5, and throughout 1 John (see the comments on 1:3; 3:23; 5:1, 10-11). It also continues the allusion to John 20:31 begun at 5:1, 5. The identity of the human Jesus with the Christ, the Son of God, and his significance for salvation, was crucial to the conflict between the author and his opponents, and it underlies these closing words (see the comments on 2:22; 4:2). As in 1:5; 4:8-10, 14-16 (see also John 1:18; 5:19-23; 10:30, 37-38; 14:7-11), the coming of the Son of God brings a revelation of the God who sent him, the *true* God, "the one who is true" (AT). This means not only the true God as distinguished from false ones (see below), but the divine reality that Johannine language calls "the truth" (see the comments on "doing the truth" in 1:6). For 1 John as well as for the Fourth Gospel (John 17:3), the knowledge of "the only true God" whom Jesus reveals gives eternal life. First John goes beyond the Gospel, however, in affirming that Christians are "in" God as well as in Jesus (see the comments on 2:6; 3:24). On the basis of the Son's revelation of God, and by being in the Son, they have a relationship with God that can be affirmed in itself. Yet this relationship is only possible for those who acknowledge the coming of God's "Son Jesus Christ."

At first glance, the one identified as the true God and eternal life at the end of verse 20 appears to be Jesus, who is called God in John 1:1, 18; 20:28, and identified with life in John 1:3-4; 11:25; 14:6; 1 John 1:2. But since the Son and the one who is true are distinguished from each other twice in this verse, it is not likely that they are identical the third time. The parallel with John 17:3 confirms that the subject is God.

The identification of God with eternal life, in fact, helps to solve the puzzle of the last verse of 1 John. Having said not a word about idols until now, the author can hardly mean to refer to them literally in his very last sentence (despite Stegemann 1985; M. J. Edwards 1989; Hills 1989). Nor could "idols" mean sin or false objects of worship in general (Schnackenburg 1992, 263-64) without some further clarification. In some way, verse 21 must relate to verses 18-20, which are about Christology and the antithesis between those born of God and the evil one, issues related to the conflict with the opponents (Ska 1979). If God's Son Jesus Christ reveals the true God, then the God proclaimed by the opponents as being revealed without the human Jesus is not true. This is the logical connection between verses 20 and 21, for the opposite of the true God is an idol.

This contrast was important in early Jewish Christian missionary preaching to non-Jews, for whom the first issue was conversion to monotheism. The readers of 1 John were probably familiar with critiques of idolatry "from the beginning," from their own conversion. The Christian mission had taken up this critique from Jewish apologetic; its ultimate roots are in the Hebrew Scriptures. "The true God" is also often called "the living God" in such contexts, just as verse 20 speaks of "the true God and eternal life." First Thessalonians 1:9 exemplifies this: In becoming Christians, the Gentile readers had "turned to God from idols, to serve a living and true God" (see also Acts 14:15; Rom 1:25; 2 Cor 6:16). Among Jewish writers, Philo contrasts pagan religion with the God who "lives forever," the God who "truly is" (*Decal.* 67, 81; see also *Spec. Leg.* 1.331-32; *Post. Cain* 166), and *Joseph and Aseneth* 11:10 contrasts idols with the "true God" and "living God" of the Hebrews. (Note also Wis 12:27; 15:1.) In the Hebrew Scriptures, Jer 10:1-16 is one of the earliest examples of this rhetoric; see also 2 Chr 15:3.

Our author's use of this traditional rhetoric continues the contrast between truth and falsehood that he has used to deprecate the opponents' Christology and other ideas (e.g., 1:6-10; 2:21-27;

4:1-6; 5:6, 10). Their Christ, who has not come in the flesh, is not the true Christ who makes known the true God and eternal life (5:11-13). Their Christology, associated with idols, belongs to the realm of the world and the evil one, from which the readers had once been converted. There is also a connection with the testing of the spirits of false prophets in 4:1-3, which is based ultimately on Deut 13:1-5; 18:20-22, where prophesying in the name of another god is condemned. Obscure as it may seem to us, the final verse of 1 John expresses a dramatic warning against falling prey to the deception against which the author has been contending all along.

◊ ◊ ◊ ◊

Though not very clear as a conclusion, this section does develop themes related to the overall theological emphases of 1 John. The "sin that leads to death," for instance, is not part of a system for classifying offenses, but is related to 1 John's fundamental concern for right Christology and mutual love. Neglect of these leads to death since it cuts one off from the source of life, Jesus, whose supreme act of love is imitated by those who have passed from death to life. The question of whether Christians can commit *any* sin, raised in such a challenging way throughout 1 John, reaches a climax in 5:16-18, where it seems to be answered both yes and no. In the end, 1 John simply leaves us with this contradiction. Yet Christianity really does hold both ideas as true, and the tension between the two may work to keep them in balance. Those who are children of God have entered into a new life; yet they remain human while living this new life, and it is important to know that if they fall back into the old ways, God, and their sisters and brothers, will stand by them.

The sharp dualism of verse 19 reflects the Johannine hostility to "the world." This sectarian enmity may have been shared by the opponents as well, given their rejection of the "flesh" of Jesus. Yet the opponents also seem to have been involved in mission to the world (4:5), and 1 John itself understands Jesus as the Savior of the world (2:2; 4:14). (On this paradox, see the comments on 2:15-17.) "The world" in the negative sense is the world in its resistance to its salvation: to the love of God, to the commandment of God to love one another, and to the true coming of God's Son. In *this* way it is in the power of the evil one, and not because it was created by the devil or is objectively ruled by the devil.

The opponents' Christology exemplifies a problem that also faced Paul and other early Christian writers, the transition of Christianity from hellenized Judaism to hellenistic culture at large. The original Johannine community had been mostly Jewish; that of 1 John was probably largely Gentile. These newer Christians would find 1 John 5:20 particularly meaningful: Jesus has given "us" Gentile Christians knowledge of the one true God. Of course, the opponents might also have said that the Son of God (but not the human Jesus) gives saving knowledge of God. The author, however, apparently saw their missionary success as the result of accommodating the gospel to the culture of "the world" (see the concluding comments on 4:1-6). He considered their spiritualized Christology a reversion to Gentile religion, to "idols." In its use of Jewish Christian missionary language, 1 John actually inverts some of the thinking that Christianity had inherited from Judaism. Instead of saying that the true God is invisible and immaterial, 1 John says that the true God is revealed in the Son, whom "we have seen with our eyes . . . and touched with our hands" (1:1), whose physical being and terrible death brought us life and let us know the true God, the God who is love.

# COMMENTARY: 2 JOHN

In its brevity and form, 2 John resembles an ordinary Greek letter. The whole would probably have fit on a single sheet of papyrus. The opening in verses 1-4 names the sender and recipients, and contains an affirmation of divine blessing and a statement of well-being. The body of the letter then follows (vv. 5-11). At the end, the writer looks forward to personal contact and sends greetings from others (vv. 12-13). Although most English translations begin the body with verse 4, the expression of happiness at the recipients' well-being there is typical of a letter *opening* (cf. Poly. *Phil.* 1), while "and now" in verse 5 (NRSV: "but now") is a common way of beginning the body (von Wahlde 1990, 63-65; Klauck 1992, 44). The theme of "truth" also unites verse 4 with verses 1-3. Some commentators suggest that verse 4 functions like the thanksgiving section of a Pauline letter (e.g., Marshall 1978, 65; Vouga 1990, 81), but this is open to question (Lieu 1986, 39-40). Verse 4 does provide a transition to the body, however, by introducing the themes of walking and the commandment. Second John has been described as a parenetic letter, that is, one that tries to persuade the audience to a course of action, using the Johannine tradition, the interests of the readers, and the author's own character as constraints (Watson 1989b, 105-8).

The ordinary letter form has been adapted in 2 John to make it a more official document, perhaps under the influence of the Pauline letters (Lieu 1986, 37-51). The initial greeting in verses 1-2 is expanded with a theological statement. Verse 3 is very similar to Paul's standard "Grace to you and peace from God our Father and the Lord Jesus Christ" (see also 1 Pet 1:2; 2 Pet 1:2; Rev 1:4); the addition of "mercy" and the omission of "our" resemble 1 Tim 1:2;

2 Tim 1:2. The substitution of "the Father's Son" for "Lord" is both more Johannine and more related to the issues with which 2 John will deal. The concluding greetings from Christians who are with the writer are also similar to other New Testament letters (besides 3 John 15, see, for example, 1 Cor 16:19; Phil 4:21-22; Titus 3:15; Heb 13:24; 1 Pet 5:13).

Second John is thus a genuine letter, but one intended to carry a kind of official authority and to encourage its readers to take certain actions. Its similarity to 1 John suggests that it addresses the same situation; perhaps it is meant to be a warning for a more distant community against the possible coming of the opponents.

**1-4:** "Elder" (v. 1) was a common title in early Christianity for members of an official *group* (e.g., Acts 14:23; 15:2-6, 22-23; 20:17; 1 Tim 5:17-19; Jas 5:14; 1 Pet 5:1). For the author to identify himself simply as "*the* elder," implying that only one person in the community was so known, is unusual. He was obviously someone in a position of honor and authority; but, as 3 John shows, this authority did not always go unquestioned. It is possible that the "elect [i.e., chosen] lady" is an individual church leader (R. B. Edwards 1996, 27-29). However, verse 13 and the plural "you" in verses 6, 8, 10, and 12 make it more likely that the "lady" and her "children" are a church and its members. (On the nature, purpose, and authorship of 2 John, see further the introduction.)

Many of the details of the first four verses function to gain the readers' goodwill for the author (Watson 1989b, 110-16). The occurrence of "truth" in each verse gives the epistolary opening a typically Johannine cast. "Walking in truth" (v. 4 [AT]) occurs in the New Testament only here and in 3 John 3-4 (see the comments on "walking" in 1 John 1:6, and compare "doing the truth" there and in John 3:21). In the context of the controversy that 2 John addresses, "walking in truth" implies agreement with the Johannine tradition, as interpreted by the elder and his party. The elder, with all who likewise know the truth, loves the "lady" and her children who walk in the truth, loves them in truth and for the sake of the eternally abiding truth (vv. 1, 2, 4): This is a very assertive claim to correctness. (It may also be significant that only *some* of the "lady's" children are said to be walking in truth.) "Truth" is indeed close to becoming merely a slogan for the group with the "right" teaching in 2 John. Yet it still retains some of its Johannine connotation of the reality of God, so that "knowing the truth" remains of central importance (cf. John 8:32; 1 John 2:21). It is this reality that abides in the Johannine Christians forever (cf. the *Spirit* of truth in John 14:16-17 and the anointing in 1 John 2:27).

Second John 3 departs from the usual form of the epistolary salutation in several ways. Such greetings generally express a wish, but the elder gives a statement of fact. This obviously indicates great confidence. It also builds on the affirmation at the end of verse 2, which accounts for the presence of "us" rather than the standard "you" in verse 3 as well. The abiding of divine truth will bring with it these other blessings for both author and readers. "Grace, mercy, peace" is practically a single entity; the Greek has a singular verb and no "and." Because of this, and since it is such a standard phrase, the individual elements probably do not carry much weight in themselves. "In truth and love" may refer to the two hallmarks of the Johannine tradition, christological faith and mutual love. It is the former that is more significant for 2 John, however, as the rather pointed inclusion of "the Father's Son" in verse 3 suggests (see the comments on vv. 5-6 below). In 1 John, the concatenation of Jesus, Christ, and Son makes up the full christological affirmation on which the author insists (see the comments on 1 John 1:3; 3:23; 5:1, 10-11, 20); it probably has the same force here.

The elder does not say how he found the "lady's" children walking in truth, whether by a visit or through messengers (such travels figure largely in both 2 and 3 John). The Greek of verse 4 says that "we have received a commandment" (NRSV: "we have been commanded"). The singular "commandment" may indicate that only one of the Johannine commandments is in view (see the comments on 1 John 3:23). If so, the reference to "truth" suggests that it is the commandment of christological faith. As in 1 John 3:22-24; 4:21–5:3, the commandment comes from God rather than from Jesus, in contrast to the Fourth Gospel (John 13:34; 14:15, 21; 15:10-17).

**5-11:** The verb of request in verse 5 is a common way to begin the body of a letter. The verse is scarcely intelligible, though, without reference to John and 1 John (suggesting that this letter was written after both of them). In John 13:34 the commandment to love one another *is* a "new commandment." First John 2:7-8 reaffirms its eschatological newness but, in words echoed here, reminds the readers that it is also not new to them, but something they have had "from the beginning" (see the comments there). This commandment has been part of the experience of the Johannine community for as long as the community has existed. Here the elder emphasizes only this traditional character, against the innovations of the opponents. (It is too much to conclude from this, however, that he has no other interest in the commandment [Lieu 1986, 76-78], especially considering the brevity and conciseness of 2 John.) Note that "love *one another*" indicates a restriction to other Christians, perhaps even to members of the Johannine community (see the comments on 1 John 2:9-11; 3:11, 23).

Second John 6 makes what is evidently an important point, but the sentence is well-nigh incomprehensible (not unlike several passages in 1 John). A very literal translation of the verse, as usually punctuated, might run: "And this is love, that we should walk according to his commandments; this is the commandment, just as you have heard from the beginning, [that/in order that] you should walk in it." The first half is at least grammatically clear; it defines love as walking according to God's commandments. That still leaves open the questions of whether this means love for other people or for God, and which commandments are in view. The second half of the verse, however, dissolves into obscurity. There are four questions. (1) Does the second "this" refer back to the preceding clause, or forward to the rest of the sentence, thus providing a definition of the commandment? (2) In the last clause of the verse, should the particle *hina* be translated "that" (expressing the content of the commandment), or "in order that" (expressing the purpose of the hearing), or as a quasi imperative addressed to the readers? (3) Does the concluding feminine singular "it" *(autē)* refer to the commandment, to love, or all the way back to the truth in verse 4? (4) Interacting with all the preceding questions, how should the verse be punctuated?

There are problems with every possible answer to each of these questions in all their combinations. If the second "this" refers backward to verse 6a, what is being identified as the commandment is left very unclear (NRSV, NAB). It remains equally unclear if "this" refers forward and *hina* is taken to mean "in order that" or to be an imperative. If "this" refers forward and *hina* means "that," the definition of the commandment becomes a tautology if "it" means the commandment; and the whole verse becomes circular if "it" means love (RSV, NIV, NJB, CEV; Smalley 1984, 326; Schnackenburg 1992, 283). There is a certain attractiveness to understanding "walk in it" to mean "walk in the truth" (von Wahlde 1990, 66-68; Klauck 1992, 49). That would contrast with the deceit in verse 7, and tie verses 4-6 together nicely. However, it requires the pronoun to refer backward over too long a distance; and if verses 5-6 begin the body of the letter, while verse 4 is part of its opening, the stretch becomes completely intolerable.

"It" must instead refer, as it most naturally should, to the commandment. Of course, verse 6a has just spoken of walking "according to" the commandments, making the change to "in" seem abrupt. But it is acceptable, since verse 6a is in any case the only place in the Johannine writings where people are said to walk "according to" rather than "in" something (cf. John 8:12; 11:9-10; 12:35; 1 John 1:6-7; 2:11; 2 John 4; 3 John 3-4). As for "this," it cannot refer forward and yield any sense. It must refer backward, which means it does not give a definition of "the commandment." Nor does it simply refer back to verse 6a, which would still leave the meaning vague. Rather, "this is the commandment" refers to the love commandment in verse 5, which the author has just defined in verse 6a as meaning walking according to God's commandments. Verse 6b says only that verse 6a is an explanation of verse 5. Punctuating with a full stop after "according to his commandments" and with nothing after "from the beginning" brings out the intended sense. Having spoken of the commandment to love one another that we have had from the beginning in verse 5, the elder says in verse 6, "And love means that we should walk according to God's commandments. *That* is the meaning of the love commandment, just as you've heard from the beginning that you should walk in it" (cf. REB; Brown 1982, 666-68).

Second John 5-6 is thus about the meaning of the love commandment. Following on verse 5, "love" in verse 6 must still mean love for one another rather than love for God. Yet the commandment is interpreted, not in terms of mutual care, but in terms of living by God's commandments in general. This rather surprising statement, which comes close to tautology itself, is quite similar to 1 John 5:2, and must have something of the same sense (see the comments there). Part of the love and faithfulness of Christians to other Christians is their faithfulness to God and God's commandments, and the one other commandment in the Johannine tradition is that of belief in Jesus as the incarnate Son of God (1 John 3:23). Since Christians' love for one another is based on the God revealed in the Incarnation (1 John 4:8-11, 14-16), they cannot fully live out this love without persisting in incarnational Christology. Also, similarly to 1 John 5:2, verse 6 thus serves to make a transition from the love commandment to that of right Christology. Since 2 John is so brief, the transition is very quick; there is no real discussion of mutual love itself to begin with. The elder simply takes it as his starting point, and uses it to move on to the issue of false Christology.

The terms in which this false Christology is condemned in verses 7-9 are essentially those found in 1 John 2:18-27; 4:1-3. Some elements prominent in 1 John are not found here: the last hour, being "of us" and "of God," knowledge, spirits. It is not even said that the opponents had "gone out from us" (see 1 John 2:19). (As in 1 John 4:1, their having "gone out into the world" [v. 7] may refer simply to their having appeared, rather than to their having left the community.) All this may be due to the brevity of 2 John as much as anything else, and the christological controversy behind it is probably at least continuous with that behind 1 John. The opponents are evidently Christians, known to the readers, and liable to appear in their community (v. 10), so that the same group, with the same Johannine roots, is probably in view.

The most important difference between the description of the opponents here and that in 1 John is in the formulation of the true christological confession. In 1 John 4:2 it was "Jesus Christ *having come* in the flesh"; here (v. 7) it is "Jesus Christ *coming* in the flesh" (a difference obscured in the NRSV; contrast NIV, NAB, REB). What 1 John calls for is apparently the confession of Jesus Christ as having brought salvation as a physical human being (see the comments there). Assuming that the same general parsing of the grammar holds good, the question is whether the use of the present rather than the perfect tense participle here is significant. Georg Strecker has suggested that the opposition in view in 2 John is not so much christological as eschatological. According to Strecker, the present tense participle implies belief in a *coming* material, millennial reign of Christ (a belief usually known as "chiliasm"). The elder takes the conservative position that Christ will reign on a physical new earth, whereas the opponents think of a spiritual or heavenly reign (Strecker 1986, 34-36; Strecker 1996, 232-36). This is a known issue in early Christianity; but the evidence for the controversy over it is a century later than the likely date of 2 John (see, e.g., Eusebius *Hist. Ecc.* 3.28.2-5).

Judith Lieu (1986, 86-87) suggests instead that the present tense participle arose from a modification of 1 John 4:2 by means of the epithet "the one who is coming" that is applied to Jesus in John 3:31; 6:14; 11:27, and is thus simply a Johannine description of Jesus without reference to any specific heresy. This is a plausible hypothesis for the origin of the wording; however, the elder does seem concerned about something specific enough to call forth a very serious warning. The use of a present tense participle to describe a past event is certainly unusual. Yet even 1 John is not consistent in its use of tenses to describe the incarnation; we also find the aorist "came" in 5:6, and a sequence of perfect and aorist, "has sent" and "sent," in 4:9-10. Second John may simply be repeating traditional Johannine language about "the one who comes" (Brown 1982, 670); or may be emphasizing the enduring significance of the Incarnation (Marshall 1978, 70-71). Even the perfect tense in 1 John 4:2 may bear something of this latter sense (see the comments there). Despite the grammatical difficulty, the overall similarity of 2 John to 1 John makes it unlikely that it envisages a radically different situation (Poly. *Phil.* 7.1 already seems to combine the two texts). At any rate, the tense of this verb is not enough to establish such a difference. Thus 2 John, like 1 John, probably opposes a teaching that denies that the human Jesus can be identified with the divine Christ, or at least denies that the human Jesus was significant for salvation.

The elder sees in the opponents the "antichrist," an eschatological deceiver. (On the origin and meaning of this term, see the comments on 1 John 2:18.) Those who guard themselves against this deception will be the ones who do not lose what "we" have worked for, but will receive their eschatological reward. This language of watchfulness and reward is not very Johannine (though see John 4:34-36; 6:27-29), and indeed is markedly different from 1 John 2:28–3:3; 4:17-18. It is more common elsewhere in early Christianity (e.g., Matt 6:1-6; Mark 13:5, 9, 23, 33; Heb 10:35; 12:25). The alternation of verb forms in verse 8 ("*you* do not lose . . . *we* have worked for . . . *you* may receive") is found in only a very small number of manuscripts, most notably the excellent Codex Vaticanus (accepted by NRSV, NJB, NAB, REB, and CEV). A number of good manuscripts have "you" consistently throughout (accepted by RSV and NIV), while the majority have "we" throughout (accepted by KJV). Both the consistent "you" and the consistent "we" probably resulted from leveling and simplifying by copyists, a tendency common in the majority of late New Testament manuscripts. The "we" here could mean the author and other church founders or authoritative tradition-bearers; but it more likely includes the readers as well, as elsewhere in 2 John (vv. 2-6, 12). The readers' watchfulness is necessary for their own sakes, but also for that of the community as a whole, both in its present existence and in its eschatological hope.

Those whom the elder opposes are said to be "going forward" (or "leading forward" [Lieu 1986, 91-93]; NRSV: "goes beyond"), rather than abiding in "the teaching of Christ" (v. 9). The latter could mean either "teaching given by Christ" (subjective genitive) or "teaching about Christ" (objective genitive); given the context, the latter is more likely. The elder evidently considers the opponents' ideas an innovation. Their "going forward" is not "walking in the truth" but "leading astray" (the basic meaning of "deceiver" in v. 7). The elder, by contrast, wants the readers to remain in what they have heard "from the beginning" (vv. 5-6; see also 1 John

2:24), that is, in the teaching about Jesus Christ "coming in flesh." Anyone who abides in this teaching "has both the Father and the Son," a somewhat unusual expression apparently referring to having the *relationship* of mutual abiding with God and Jesus (see the comments on 1 John 2:23; see also 1 John 5:12).

The primary action to which 2 John exhorts its readers is the refusal of hospitality to the opponents (vv. 10-11). Harsh as this sounds, its point becomes clear when we recognize that in early Christianity, hospitality was not only a primary means of expressing love, but was also essential to traveling missionaries and teachers. Receiving people into one's house meant offering them material aid, and perhaps also a place to speak to a congregation meeting as a house-church. Hospitality thus implied not just love and generosity, but the provision of a base for mission, as 3 John 5-8 shows. (See also Acts 16:14-15; Rom 12:13; 15:23-24; 16:1-2; Titus 3:13; Heb 13:1-2; *Did.* 11-12. For the roots of this practice in the mission of Jesus, see Mark 6:10; Luke 10:5-7.) By forbidding hospitality, the elder hoped to hinder the spread of the opponents' teaching (cf. Rom 16:17; 2 Thess 3:6-12; *Did.* 11:1-2; Ign. *Eph.* 7:1; 9:1; Ign. *Smyrn.* 4:1; regarding doctrinal and other tests for Christian teachers, see the comments on 1 John 4:1-6). Pheme Perkins (1983, 635-37) has shown that the "participation" *(koinōneō)* deprecated in verse 11 implies a formal partnership, a sense that the term apparently had in the Pauline mission (Phil 1:5; 1 Cor 9:23). The elder's claim that even offering people a greeting *(chairein,* "hello" or "welcome") brings one into partnership with them may seem extreme, but it reflects the reality of the early Christian mission.

**12-13:** The endings of 2 and 3 John are very similar. Both indicate that the elder would prefer to make a personal visit rather than put everything into writing. This, however, was an epistolary convention and so need not be taken with full seriousness; it does not tell us anything about the relation of 2 John to 1 John (Brown 1982, 693-95). "So that our joy may be complete" (v. 12) is reminiscent of 1 John 1:4, and also of John 3:29; 15:11; 16:24; 17:13. The usage here is not as highly charged as elsewhere, however. The reference is not to eschatological joy but to the pleasure of human contact in contrast to the remoteness of written communication. It is the sort of commonplace expected at the end of a Greek letter, expressed here in Johannine terminology. It remains just possible, though, that by using this expression the elder meant to suggest that the joy in their meeting would be a foretaste of that ultimate joy, because they were members of the eschatological community.

◊ ◊ ◊ ◊

Brief as it is, 2 John raises several theological issues. As in 1 John (though in a less profound way), the love commandment is related to right christological belief. The underlying theological structure is probably the same: Christian love, the love that God is, was revealed and exemplified in the human Jesus. After his opening appeal to the commandment of love, the elder's prohibition of hospitality to the opponents seems starkly inconsistent, and in sharp contrast to 1 John 3:17. (In 3 John 9-10, he complains of similar tactics being employed against himself!) It is perhaps some help to recall that this is not a refusal of charity to the needy, but an attempt to block false teaching. Hospitality was not only an expression of love, as it might be today, but a mission strategy, and the elder was concerned to prevent his opponents from spreading a Christology that he regarded as itself a threat to the realization of Christian love.

The elder's position seems fiercely conservative: Do not go forward, but abide in the tradition. As in 1 John, however, it is not tradition as such, but continuity with the truth that counts. The problem is not change itself ("progress," in our sense, was scarcely known in the ancient world), but the abandonment of incarnational Christology, of the revelation of God in the human Jesus. Yet Judith Lieu rightly notes that the issues in 2 John are expressed differently than in 1 John. It is not a matter of testing spirits and abiding in Jesus or in God, but of remaining loyal to a *teaching*, a doctrine, for fear of losing a reward (Lieu 1986, 83, 89-90, 93-94). Even allowing more than Lieu does for 2 John's brevity and the way in which it summarizes themes rather than fully unfolding them, this is significant. Whether by the same author in the same situation or not, 2 John does move a step closer to a focus on tradition for its own sake, something that can be defined and preserved in a more static way than even 1 John seems to allow.

# COMMENTARY: 3 JOHN

Even more than 2 John, 3 John has a form typical of ancient personal letters. The general prayer for blessing and health (v. 2) is especially characteristic. Its opening does not have the adaptations found in most New Testament letters (see the literary analysis of 2 John), though "whom I love in truth" (v. 1) and "just as it is well with your soul" (v. 2) add a Johannine religious touch. Especially in comparison with 2 John, 3 John is a truly personal, unofficial letter (Lieu 1986, 37-51). Its one remarkable feature is the lack of an actual greeting, either the usual Greek *chairein* or an early Christian form similar to 2 John 3.

Because of this personal nature, 3 John is less amenable than 2 John to an analysis in terms of ancient rhetoric (as in Watson 1989c; contrast Klauck 1990, 221-24). The structure of the letter is given by the three addresses to Gaius as "beloved" (vv. 2, 5, 11). The first of these introduces the wish for well-being and the compliments typical of Greek letter openings. These general compliments are then made more specific in the body of the letter (vv. 5-12) by praise for Gaius's hospitality (vv. 5-8), which is contrasted with the inhospitality of Diotrephes (vv. 9-10). The encouragement to imitate good and not evil in verse 11 grows out of this contrast, and also introduces the commendation of Demetrius as one who is known to do good. In its closing, 3 John closely resembles 2 John: The writer anticipates a personal visit and exchanges greetings (vv. 13-15; see the literary analysis of 2 John, and the comments on 2 John 12-13).

**The Situation:** Like many letters that use a conventional form, 3 John is clearly addressed to a specific situation. That situation was much better known to its author and its original recipient than it is to us, of course, and has therefore been the subject of much scholarly discussion. (For details of the view adopted here, see the introduction.)

Four persons are mentioned by name or title in 3 John. The identity of the elder (v. 1) is discussed in the introduction and the comments on 2 John 1. Gaius (v. 1) was a common Roman name, borne by three men named elsewhere in the New Testament, natives respectively of Macedonia (Acts 19:29), Derbe (Acts 20:4), and Corinth (Rom 16:23; 1 Cor 1:14). It is not likely that any of these is the recipient of 3 John, especially if the letter is to be dated around or after 100 CE. The identity of Demetrius (v. 12), whom the elder commends to Gaius's imitation and apparently his hospitality (vv. 5-8), is equally unknown. (Despite the intriguing presence of both a Gaius and a Demetrius in Ephesus—the traditional place of writing for 3 John—in Acts 19:23-41, there is no reason to think that they are the same, especially since that Demetrius would have needed quite a different recommendation to that Gaius.) The fourth individual, Diotrephes (v. 9), will be discussed below.

Besides these four, note also the *adelphoi* ("brothers," or "brothers and sisters") in verses 3, 5, and 10, probably all referring to the same group. (The NRSV translates *adelphoi* as "friends," which it also uses, more naturally, for *philoi* in v. 15.) These brothers and sisters are the source of the elder's information, and their treatment is at the center of the problem addressed by 3 John.

This problem was fundamentally a controversy between Diotrephes and the elder, as a result of which the elder sought Gaius's help. Some believe that this controversy was about church polity, seeing in either the elder or Diotrephes the beginnings of the monarchical episcopacy. (The Greek of v. 9 specifies that Diotrephes likes to be first "over them," i.e., the members of the church, which is not reflected in many English translations.) But in fact, neither man had any real authority over the other, and it is not clear that the struggle was about structural issues rather than personal power. Another possibility often raised is that the dispute was doctrinal, as in 1 and 2 John. But if Diotrephes and the elder had been on opposite sides in such a dispute, the latter would surely have said so openly.

Conceivably, Diotrephes was trying to remain neutral, by refusing the elder's messengers and those of the other side as well. Perhaps, combining the two possibilities, Diotrephes took the measures deprecated in 3 John in an attempt to create an ecclesiastical structure that could deal with doctrinal conflicts. But the lack of overt reference to the dispute behind 1 and 2 John more likely means that 3 John has no relation to it at all. Diotrephes is accused of personal ambition, insulting the elder, and interfering with the elder's communications with "the church" by refusing to show hospitality himself and by exerting his power so as to prevent others from showing it (vv. 9-10). This is as much as we really know.

As for Gaius's position, he seems neither to belong to "the church" headed by Diotrephes (since the elder must inform him of its affairs) nor to have any influence over it. He is, however, on good terms with the elder, is indeed one of his "children" (v. 4), though the elder seeks to persuade rather than to command him. He has evidently received the elder's messengers' hospitably once, and 3 John is a request that he do so again, following their rebuff by Diotrephes. He is not asked to intervene in the conflict. Rather, the purpose of 3 John is to encourage Gaius's hospitality, perhaps especially to Demetrius (v. 12), whom it contrasts with Diotrephes as a model worthy of Gaius's imitation.

**Vocabulary:** Third John contains only a relatively small amount of Johannine language, primarily in the references to love, truth, testimony, and God in verses 1, 3-4, 6, 8, 11, and 12. "Whom I love in truth" (v. 1) is like 2 John 1 (see also 1 John 3:18); "walk in the truth" (v. 3) occurs only in 2 John 4 elsewhere in the New Testament (on "walking," see the comments on 1 John 1:6). (NRSV and NIV expand "your truth" in v. 3 to "your *faithfulness* to the truth.") These references to "truth" lead some to see the christological dispute of 2 John in 3 John as well. But Christology is not mentioned in 3 John, nor need "truth" be shorthand for it. Rather, Gaius's "truth," the evidence that his soul is well, is the same as his "love": it is his hospitality, which is attested in the same way (v. 6). The different contexts in the two letters define two different meanings for "walking in truth." Here it refers to deeds rather than doctrine, and so is comparable to "doing the truth" in 1 John 1:6; John 3:21. Nevertheless, this hospitality to traveling missionaries is also essential to the spreading of true doctrine (see the comments on vv. 5-8 below), and Gaius thus becomes a coworker with the truth (v. 8). As in 2 John, the concept of "truth" seems to be slipping from its Johannine sense of "divine reality" toward being merely a slogan for belonging to the right party in a conflict (see the comments on 2 John 1-4); yet it remains linked to actions that accord with the revelation of God as love in Jesus.

The language of testimony and witness is very important in the Gospel of John and in 1 John, but there we read of testimony to Jesus (or given by Jesus) rather than to individual Christians. The usage here is more like that in ordinary letters of recommendation, when someone's hospitality is to be attested. This, of course, is precisely the point in verses 3, 6 (see further the comments on verse 12).

Third John 4 is the only place in the Johannine writings where *tekna* is used to refer to the reader as one of the author's "children." In John and 1 John *tekna* refers mainly to children of God, and in 2 John to the "children" of (probably) symbolic figures; the contrast between 2 John 4 and 3 John 4 is especially striking. When 1 John addresses the readers as "children," it uses two different words, *teknia* and *paidia* (see the comments on 1 John 2:12-14; see also John 13:33; 21:5). Third John's usage is more like that of Paul (e.g., 1 Cor 4:14; Gal 4:19) and the Pastoral Letters (e.g., 1 Tim 1:2, 18; Titus 1:4). Another term, "church" *(ekklēsia)*, is used only in 3 John 6, 9-10 in the Johannine literature. As frequently in Paul's letters, it refers to a congregation, a house-church, not to the church as an institution. Similarly, 3 John uses missionary language that is not Johannine, but is common elsewhere in the New Testament and other early Christian writings: "send on," "for the sake of the name," and "co-workers" (see the comments below).

Thus the language of 3 John combines a few distinctively Johannine features with others that belong to the wider Christian sphere, in a form that is simply that of an ordinary Greek letter. Though this hardly proves that 3 John has a different author, it does set it somewhat apart, despite its similarities to 2 John in other respects.

In fact, perhaps due to its occasion, it is more the non-Johannine and even non-Christian language and forms than the Johannine ones that carry the message of the letter (Lieu 1986, 123).

**5-12:** Whoever Gaius was, he obviously had the material resources necessary to show hospitality to the brothers and sisters (vv. 5-8). The formula "You will do well to . . . for they . . . " (vv. 6-7) is very common in letters of recommendation (Kim 1972, 62-66, 86-87; see Ign. *Smyrn.* 10:1). The elder's request that he "send them on" (v. 6) means not just to see them off but to give them concrete assistance (Acts 15:3; Rom 15:24; 1 Cor 16:6, 11; 2 Cor 1:16; Titus 3:13; Poly. *Phil.* 1.1). The nature of their present journey is clear from its being "for the sake of the name" (v. 7; NRSV margin). Though the name of Jesus is important in John and 1 John (see the comments on 1 John 2:12), "the name" as such is not a Johannine expression, and in this absolute usage is rare elsewhere in the New Testament. It is especially in the story of the early Christian mission in the book of Acts that we read of Christians preaching, suffering, and doing miracles in Jesus' name, and where we find "the name" used to symbolize this on one occasion (Acts 5:41). The travelers mentioned in 3 John must therefore be on mission. That is why they accept nothing from nonbelievers (v. 7; literally "Gentiles," a term inherited from the church's Jewish origins). Christians who assist them thus become "co-workers with the truth" (v. 8). "Truth" is a natural Johannine term for the gospel, and "co-workers" is reminiscent of many contexts related to the Pauline mission (e.g., 1 Cor 16:16; 2 Cor 8:23; Phil 2:25; 4:3; 1 Thess 3:2; Phlm 1, 24). Gaius's hospitality is thus not only a demonstration of his love but a means of participating in the spreading of the gospel, just as the refusal of hospitality in 2 John 10-11 is a refusal to participate in the spreading of false teaching. (See further the comments there on the importance of hospitality in the mission of early Christianity.)

The earlier journey referred to in verses 9-10 may not have been exclusively a missionary one, since it included a letter to "the church." It is possible, of course, that this letter was 2 John, but there is no proof of this, nor that the letter had to do with the christological dispute. It was probably not a simple letter of recommendation, however, since the letter itself was rejected and not just the messengers. The plurals "us" and "we" in verses 9-10, 12 do not necessarily indicate that the elder wrote as part of the Johannine tradition-bearing group (see the comments on 1 John 1:1-4), but they do suggest a sense of authority. In any case, he wished to communicate some message to a congregation, and Diotrephes frustrated this wish by refusing the letter and the messengers who brought it, thereby refusing the elder himself. His further actions, preventing other members of the congregation from offering their hospitality, amount to using the tactics of 2 John 10-11 against the elder, though it is not certain who originated these tactics, since the chronological relationship between 2 and 3 John is unclear.

The word translated "welcome" in verse 10 *(epidechetai)* is also used in verse 9, where it is sometimes translated "acknowledge our authority." This is more than the word means, however (Malherbe 1983, 106-7). In Greco-Roman diplomacy it commonly referred to the reception of an envoy (see 1 Macc 10:46; 12:8, 43; 14:23), and something like this is the sense here (NJB: "refuses to accept us"). The rejection of the emissaries meant the rejection of the elder, but this tells us nothing about Diotrephes' motivation, which may not have had anything to do with authority. According to verse 10, Diotrephes multiplied this insult by spreading malicious nonsense about the elder (literally "babbling against us with evil words").

In verse 11 the elder turns from Diotrephes to make a final exhortation to Gaius. Distinguishing people who are from God from those who have not seen God on the basis of conduct is reminiscent of a major theme in 1 John (2:29; 3:6, 10; 4:7). It must be noted, however, that 1 John speaks of seeing *Jesus,* and that the usual idea is that *no one* has seen God (John 1:18; 5:37; 6:46; 1 John 4:12, 20). The elder seems to imply that those who do good have seen God, perhaps because in this way they continue the revelation of God in the mutual love of Christians (see the comments on 1 John 4:12).

The exhortation to imitate good rather than evil (v. 11) is an obvious commonplace in moral rhetoric, which in antiquity made much use of positive and negative examples. Such language, however, is more common elsewhere in early Christianity than in the

Johannine writings (e.g., 1 Cor 10:1-13; 2 Thess 3:6-13; Heb 13:7; *1 Clem.* 17-18). Even the many exhortations to imitate Jesus in 1 John do not use the verb "imitate." Similarly, the verbs "do good" and "do evil" occur only in John 5:29 elsewhere in the Johannine writings (see also 1 Pet 2:14-15; 3:17; *Herm. Sim.* 9.18.1-2). In *Herm. Man.* 8.10, "doing good" is equated with hospitality. Given what has preceded, Gaius is thus partly being urged to follow his own hospitable example.

The general contrast in verse 11, however, also allows the elder to balance the well-attested Demetrius against the problematic Diotrephes. What is said of Demetrius is often considered to be a commendation of him to Gaius's hospitality, perhaps as the bearer of 3 John (e.g., Malherbe 1983, 105-6; Malina 1986, 187). Letters of recommendation were a necessity for unknown travelers claiming to be Christian workers (Acts 18:27; Rom 16:1-2; 1 Cor 16:3; 2 Cor 3:1; 8:16-24; see Stowers 1986, 153-65). However, Judith Lieu (1986, 117-19) suggests that the specific terminology in verse 12, of attestation rather than commendation, is not typical of such letters, and that Demetrius is really the example of well-doing whom Gaius is to imitate. Hebrews 11:2; *1 Clem.* 17.1-2; 18.1 may bear this out; on the other hand, a *Johannine* letter of recommendation might well use the language of testimony. Elements of both kinds of rhetoric seem to be combined here, as the elder both commends Demetrius to Gaius's hospitality and presents him as an example for Gaius to follow.

Exactly how "the truth itself" (v. 12) testified to Demetrius is hard to know. The reference could be to Demetrius's manner of life as being in accord with truth (similarly to Gaius in vv. 3-4); to his attestation by the Johannine community as those who know the truth; to his support of the elder's position in the conflict; or even, less probably, to an attestation inspired by Christ (see John 14:6) or the Spirit (see 1 John 5:6). The expression resembles a vague Greek commonplace (Klauck 1992, 117). "You know that our testimony is true" is certainly an allusion to John 5:31-32; 19:35; 21:24. The use of such theologically loaded Johannine language for so relatively trivial a purpose is a bit surprising. Perhaps the seriousness of the situation required serious words; or perhaps it is a mark of the intensity of the Johannine community or of this author to use such language even for mundane purposes. It is equally possible, however, that in 3 John even important Johannine vocabulary is used merely for slogans.

**13-15:** Though the concluding exchange of greetings is typical of New Testament letters, the wish for peace to the reader is not (found only in Eph 6:23; 1 Pet 5:14); such a wish usually comes at the beginning (see the literary analysis of 2 John). In a Johannine context, one is reminded of John 20:19, 21, 26. "Friends" (*philoi*, v. 15) is not used anywhere else in the New Testament as a designation for fellow Christians in this way (though see Acts 27:3); it is a notable change from the earlier "brothers and sisters" (*adelphoi*, vv. 3, 5, 10; also rendered "friends" in NRSV). Again the Johannine context might bring to mind John 11:11; 15:13-15; but greetings to friends "by name" at the end of a letter are so commonplace as to be unremarkable. These usages probably exemplify not Johannine theology so much as an early Christian author writing in a context more private than official, using the conventions of ordinary Greek letters.

◊ ◊ ◊ ◊

The complete lack of theological discussion in 3 John accords with its private and personal character. Its references to God are purely formulaic (vv. 6, 11), and it makes no mention of Jesus except indirectly ("the name," v. 7). Yet 3 John is not entirely without theological interest. We see Christian love and truth not as abstractions here, but linked in concrete ways to the spreading of the gospel and to practical life in the church. We also see that church politics is nothing new. The radicalism of the Johannine tradition brought with it the risk of an especially splintered and polarized politics, with theological profundities degenerating into mere slogans. Far from being an age of pristine harmony, New Testament Christianity already shows an all-too-human face. Third John presents an early instance of the church's perpetual need, and occasional failure, to treat such circumstances in light of the claim on which the other Johannine epistles insist, that the God of love has been revealed in human flesh to do away with human sin.

# SELECT BIBLIOGRAPHY

## WORKS CITED IN THE TEXT
### (EXCLUDING COMMENTARIES)

Antoniotti, Louise-Marie. 1988. "Structure littéraire et sens de la Première Épître de Jean." *RevThom* 88:5-35.

Becker, Jürgen. 1969. "Aufbau, Schichtung und theologiegeschichtliche Stellung des Gebetes in Johannes 17." *ZNW* 60:56-83.

———. 1970. "Die Abschiedsreden Jesu im Johannesevangelium." *ZNW* 61:215-46.

Beutler, Johannes. 1989. "Krise und Untergang der johanneischen Gemeinde: Das Zeugnis der Johannesbriefe." In *The New Testament in Early Christianity: La réception des écrits néotestamentaires dans le christianisme primitif,* edited by Jean-Marie Sevrin, 85-103. BETL 86. Louvain: Leuven University Press.

Blank, Josef. 1984. "Die Irrlehrer des Ersten Johannesbriefes." *Kairos,* n.s., 26:166-93.

Bogart, John. 1977. *Orthodox and Heretical Perfectionism in the Johannine Community as Evident in the First Epistle of John.* SBLDS 33. Missoula, MT: Scholars Press.

Boyer, James L. 1988. "Relative Clauses in the Greek New Testament: A Statistical Study." *Grace Theological Journal* 9:233-56.

Braun, Herbert. 1951. "Literar-Analyse und theologische Schichtung im ersten Johannesbriefe." *ZTK* 48:262-92.

Brown, Raymond E. 1979. *The Community of the Beloved Disciple.* New York: Paulist.

Brox, Norbert. 1984. " 'Doketismus'—eine Problemanzeige." *ZKG* 95:301-14.

Bultmann, Rudolf. 1967a. "Analyse des ersten Johannesbriefes." In *Exegetica: Aufsätze zur Erforschung des Neuen Testaments,* edited by Erich Dinkler, 105-23. Tübingen: Mohr-Siebeck. Originally published in *Festgabe für Adolf Jülicher zum 70. Geburtstag.* Tübingen: Mohr-Siebeck, 1927, 138-58.

———. 1967b. "Die kirchliche Redaktion des ersten Johannesbriefes." In *Exegetica: Aufsätze zur Erforschung des Neuen Testaments,* edited by

Erich Dinkler, 381-93. Tübingen: Mohr-Siebeck. Originally published in *In Memoriam Ernst Lohmeyer* (Stuttgart: Evangelisches Verlagswerk, 1951), 189-201.

Conzelmann, Hans. 1954. " 'Was von Anfang war.' " In *Neutestamentliche Studien für Rudolf Bultmann zu seinem siebzigsten Gebürtstag,* edited by Walther Eltester, 194-201. BZNW 21. Berlin: Töpelmann.

Culpepper, R. Alan. 1975. *The Johannine School: An Evaluation of the Johannine-school Hypothesis Based on an Investigation of the Nature of Ancient Schools.* SBLDS 26. Missoula, MT: Scholars Press.

Dahl, Nils Alstrup. 1964. "Der Erstgeborene Satans und der Vater des Teufels (Polyk. 7 1 und Joh 8 44)." In *Apophoreta: Festschrift für Ernst Haenchen zu seinem 70. Geburtstag,* edited by Walther Eltester, 70-84. BZNW 30. Berlin: Töpelmann.

de Boer, Martinus C. 1991. "The Death of Jesus Christ and His Coming in the Flesh (1 John 4:2)." *NovT* 33:326-46.

Dodd, C. H. 1937. "The First Epistle of John and the Fourth Gospel." *BJRL* 21:129-56.

Donfried, Karl Paul. 1977. "Ecclesiastical Authority in 2-3 John." In *L'Évangile de Jean: sources, rédaction, théologie,* edited by M. de Jonge, 325-33. BETL 44. Gembloux: Duculot.

du Preez, J. 1975. " 'Sperma Autou' in I John 3:9." *Neot* 9:105-12.

Edwards, M. J. 1989. "Martyrdom and the First Epistle of John." *NovT* 31:164-71.

Edwards, Ruth B. 1996. *The Johannine Epistles.* New Testament Guides. Sheffield, England: Sheffield Academic Press.

Ehrman, Bart D. 1988. "1 John 4:3 and the Orthodox Corruption of Scripture." *ZNW* 79:221-43.

Feuillet, André. 1972. "Étude structurale de la première épître de saint Jean: Comparaison avec le quatrième évangile: La structure fondamentale de la vie chrétienne selon saint Jean." *In Neues Testament und Geschichte: Historisches Geschehen und Deutung im Neuen Testament: Oscar Cullmann zum 70. Geburtstag,* edited by Heinrich Baltensweiler and Bo Reicke, 307-27. Zürich: Theologischer Verlag.

Gaba, Octavius A. 1995. "Symbols of Revelation: The Darkness of the Hebrew Yahweh and the Light of the Greek Logos." In *The Recovery of Black Presence: An Interdisciplinary Exploration: Essays in Honor of Dr. Charles B. Copher,* edited by Randall C. Bailey and Jacquelyn Grant, 143-58. Nashville: Abingdon.

Grayston, Kenneth. 1981. "The Meaning of PARAKLĒTOS." *JSNT* 13:67-82.

Haas, C., M. de Jonge, and J. L. Swellengrebel. 1972. *A Translator's Handbook on the Letters of John.* Helps for Translators. London: United Bible Societies.

Harnack, Adolf von. 1897. *Über den dritten Johannesbrief.* TU 15/3b. Leipzig: J. C. Hinrichs.

Heise, Jürgen. 1967. *Bleiben: Menein in den Johanneischen Schriften.* HUT 8. Tübingen: Mohr-Siebeck.

Hills, Julian V. 1989. " 'Little Children, Keep Yourselves from Idols': 1 John 5:21 Reconsidered." *CBQ* 51:285-310.

———. 1991. "A Genre for 1 John." In *The Future of Early Christianity: Essays in Honor of Helmut Koester,* edited by Birger A. Pearson, A. Thomas Kraabel, George W. E. Nickelsburg, and Norman R. Petersen, 367-77. Minneapolis: Fortress.

Käsemann, Ernst. 1951. "Ketzer und Zeuge: Zum johanneischen Verfasserproblem." *ZTK* 48:292-311.

———. 1968. *The Testament of Jesus: A Study of the Gospel of John in the Light of Chapter 17.* Philadelphia: Fortress.

Kim, Chan-Hie. 1972. *Form and Structure of the Familiar Greek Letter of Recommendation.* SBLDS 4. Missoula, MT: Society of Biblical Literature.

Klauck, Hans-Josef. 1988. "Internal Opponents: The Treatment of the Secessionists in the First Epistle of John." Translated by Robert Nowell. In *Truth and Its Victims,* edited by Wim Beuken, Sean Freyne, and Anton Weiler, 55-65. Concilium 200. Edinburgh: T & T Clark.

———. 1989. "Gemeinde ohne Amt? Erfahrungen mit der Kirche in den johanneischen Schriften." In *Gemeinde—Amt—Sakrament: Neutestamentliche Perspektiven,* 195-222. Würzburg: Echter Verlag. Originally in *BZ* 29 (1985): 193-220.

———. 1990. "Zur rhetorischen Analyse der Johannesbriefe." *ZNW* 81:205-24.

Klein, Günter. 1971. " 'Das wahre Licht scheint schon.' Beobachtungen zur Zeit- und Geschichtserfahrung einer urchristlichen Schule." *ZTK* 68:261-326.

Kubo, Sakae. 1969. "I John 3:9: Absolute or Habitual?" *AUSS* 7 (January): 47-56.

Law, Robert. 1914. *The Tests of Life: A Study of the First Epistle of St. John.* 3d ed. Edinburgh: T & T Clark.

Lieu, Judith M. 1981. " 'Authority to Become Children of God': A Study of 1 John." *NovT* 23 (July): 210-28.

———. 1986. *The Second and Third Epistles of John: History and Background.* Studies of the New Testament and Its World. Edinburgh: T & T Clark.

———. 1991. *The Theology of the Johannine Epistles.* New Testament Theology. Cambridge: Cambridge University Press.

Malatesta, Edward. 1978. *Interiority and Covenant: A Study of* einai en *and* menein en *in the First Letter of Saint John.* AnBib 69. Rome: Biblical Institute Press.

———. 1984. "*Tēn agapen hēn echei ho theos en hēmin:* A Note on 1 John 4:16a." In *The New Testament Age: Essays in Honor of Bo Reicke,* edited by Willam C. Weinrich. Vol. 2. 301-11. Macon, GA: Mercer University Press.

Malherbe, Abraham J. 1983. "Hospitality and Inhospitality in the Church." In *Social Aspects of Early Christianity,* 2d ed., rev. and enl., 92-112. Philadelphia: Fortress. Originally "The Inhospitality of Diotrephes," in *God's Christ and His People,* edited by Jacob Jervell and Wayne A. Meeks (Oslo: Universitetsforlaget, 1977), 222-32.

Malina, Bruce J. 1986. "The Received View and What It Cannot Do: III John and Hospitality." *Semeia* 35:171-94.

Merritt, H. Wayne. 1993. *In Word and Deed: Moral Integrity in Paul.* Emory Studies in Early Christianity 1. New York: Peter Lang.

Merton, Thomas. 1961. *New Seeds of Contemplation.* New York: New Directions.

Miranda, José Porfirio. 1977. *Being and the Messiah: The Message of St. John.* Maryknoll, NY: Orbis.

Morgen, Michèle. 1987. "L'évangile interprété par l'épître: Jean et I Jean." *Foi et vie* 86 (September): 59-70.

Nauck, Wolfgang. 1957. *Die Tradition und der Charakter des ersten Johannesbriefes.* WUNT 3. Tübingen: Mohr-Siebeck.

O'Neill, J. C. 1966. *The Puzzle of 1 John: A New Examination of Origins.* London: SPCK.

Painter, John. 1986. "The 'Opponents' in 1 John." *NTS* 32:48-71.

Perkins, Pheme. 1983. "Koinōnia in 1 John 1:3-7: The Social Context of Division in the Johannine Letters." *CBQ* 45:631-41.

Piper, Otto A. 1947. "1 John and the Didache of the Primitive Church." *JBL* 66:437-51.

Poythress, Vern S. 1984. "Testing for Johannine Authorship by Examining the Use of Conjunctions." *WTJ* 46:350-69.

Pratscher, Wilhelm. 1976. "Gott ist grösser als unser Herz: Zur Interpretation von 1. Joh. 3,19f." *TZ* 32 (September–October): 272-81.

Rensberger, David. 1988. *Johannine Faith and Liberating Community.* Philadelphia: Westminster.

———. 1992. "Love for One Another and Love for Enemies in the Gospel of John." In *The Love of Enemy and Nonretaliation in the New Testament,* edited by Willard M. Swartley, 297-313. Louisville: Westminster/John Knox.

Rese, Martin. 1985. "Das Gebot der Bruderliebe in den Johannesbriefen." *TZ* 41:44-58.

Robinson, John A. T. 1962. "The Destination and Purpose of the Johannine Epistles." In *Twelve New Testament Studies,* 126-38. SBT 34. London: SCM. Originally in NTS 7 (1960–1961): 56-65.

Rusam, Dietrich. 1993. *Die Gemeinschaft der Kinder Gottes: Das Motiv der Gotteskindschaft und die Gemeinden der johanneischen Briefe.* BWANT 133. Stuttgart: Kohlhammer.

Schnackenburg, Rudolf. 1971. "Wahrheit in Glaubenssätzen: Überlegungen nach dem ersten Johannesbrief." In *Zum Problem Unfehlbarkeit: Antworten auf die Anfrage von Hans Küng,* edited by Karl Rahner, 134-47. QD 54. Freiburg: Herder.

Scholer, David M. 1975. "Sins Within and Sins Without: An Interpretation of 1 John 5:16-17." In *Current Issues in Biblical and Patristic Interpretation: Studies in Honor of Merrill C. Tenney Presented by His Former Students,* edited by Gerald F. Hawthorne, 230-46. Grand Rapids, MI: Eerdmans.

Segovia, Fernando F. 1987. "Recent Research in the Johannine Letters." *RelSRev* 13:132-39.

Ska, J.-L. 1979. " 'Petits enfants, prenez garde aux idoles': 1 Jn 5,21." *NRT* 101:860-74.

Stegemann, Ekkehard. 1985. " 'Kindlein, hütet euch vor den Götterbildern!': Erwägungen zum Schluss des 1. Johannesbriefes." *TZ* 41:284-94.

Stowers, Stanley K. 1986. *Letter Writing in Greco-Roman Antiquity.* Library of Early Christianity. Philadelphia: Westminster.

Strecker, Georg. 1986. "Die Anfänge der johanneischen Schule." *NTS* 32:31-47.

Swadling, Harry C. 1982. "Sin and Sinlessness in 1 John." *SJT* 35:205-11.

Thomas, John Christopher. 1995. "The Order of the Composition of the Johannine Epistles." *NovT* 37:68-75.

Vitrano, Steven P. 1987. "The Doctrine of Sin in 1 John." *AUSS* 25:123-31.

von Wahlde, Urban C. 1990. *The Johannine Commandments: 1 John and the Struggle for the Johannine Tradition.* Theological Inquiries. New York: Paulist.

Watson, Duane F. 1989a. "1 John 2:12-14 as *Distributio, Conduplicatio,* and *Expolitio:* A Rhetorical Understanding." *JSNT* 35:97-110.

———. 1989b. "A Rhetorical Analysis of 2 John According to Greco-Roman Conventions." *NTS* 35:104-30.

———. 1989c. "A Rhetorical Analysis of 3 John: A Study in Epistolary Rhetoric." *CBQ* 51:479-501.

———. 1993. "Amplification Techniques in 1 John: The Interaction of Rhetorical Style and Invention." *JSNT* 51:99-123.

Webster, J. B. 1986. "The Imitation of Christ." *TynBul* 37:95-120.

Wengst, Klaus. 1976. *Häresie und Orthodoxie im Spiegel des ersten Johannesbriefes.* Gütersloh: Gerd Mohn.

Whitacre, Rodney A. 1982. *Johannine Polemic: The Role of Tradition and Theology.* SBLDS 67. Chico, CA: Scholars Press.

Yoder, John Howard. 1972. *The Politics of Jesus.* Grand Rapids, MI: Eerdmans.

## COMMENTARIES (BOTH CITED AND NOT CITED)

Bonnard, Pierre. 1983. *Les Épîtres johanniques.* CNT, 2d ser. 13c. Geneva: Labor et Fides. — French Protestant commentary that consistently uses the conflict with the opponents as the key to the epistles, including 3 John.

Brooke, A. E. 1912. *A Critical and Exegetical Commentary on the Johannine Epistles.* ICC. Edinburgh: T & T Clark. — Still very useful for its detailed and learned treatment of the Greek text, including matters of textual criticism.

Brown, Raymond E. 1982. *The Epistles of John.* AB 30. Garden City, NY: Doubleday. — Best and most comprehensive critical commentary on the epistles. Hypothesis that the epistles originated in a dispute over interpretation of Johannine tradition has been very influential.

Bultmann, Rudolf. 1973. *The Johannine Epistles.* Translated by R. Philip O'Hara, assisted by Lane C. McGaughy and Robert W. Funk. Edited by Robert W. Funk. Hermeneia. Philadelphia: Fortress. — Translated from German. Not as influential as Bultmann's work on the Gospel of John, especially in its theories of source and redaction, but has characteristically penetrating theological insights.

Dodd, C. H. 1946. *The Johannine Epistles.* MNTC. New York: Harper & Row. — Learned but readable treatment by a great British Johannine scholar. Exegetical and theological reflections in light of the hellenistic religious context.

Grayston, Kenneth. 1984. *The Johannine Epistles*. NCB. Grand Rapids, MI: Eerdmans. — Concise, but with some detailed exegetical discussions. Proposes an original theory that 1 John is earlier than John and was directed against opponents claiming a Spirit-anointing equal to that of Jesus.

Houlden, J. L. 1973. *A Commentary on the Johannine Epistles*. HNTC. New York: Harper & Row. — Fairly brief, but a thorough treatment; balanced and accessible.

Johnson, Thomas F. 1993. *1, 2, and 3 John*. New International Biblical Commentary. Peabody, MA: Hendrickson. — Reliable exegesis based on up-to-date scholarship, intended for lay Bible students.

Klauck, Hans-Josef. 1991. *Der erste Johannesbrief*. EKKNT 23/1. Zürich: Benziger Verlag; Neukirchen-Vluyn: Neukirchener Verlag. —Very comprehensive, thorough, and balanced two-volume treatment of the epistles, including discussion of the impact of each passage on later Christian theology.

———. 1992. *Der zweite und dritte Johannesbrief*. EKKNT 23/2. Zürich: Benziger Verlag; Neukirchen-Vluyn: Neukirchener Verlag. —Very comprehensive, thorough, and balanced two-volume treatment of the epistles, including discussion of the impact of each passage on later Christian theology.

Kysar, Robert. 1986. *I, II, III John*. Augsburg Commentary on the New Testament. Minneapolis: Augsburg. — Brief but critically informed interpretation for laypeople, students, and pastors.

Marshall, I. Howard. 1978. *The Epistles of John*. NICNT. Grand Rapids, MI: Eerdmans. — Readable but thorough, with thoughtful treatment of theological issues from an evangelical point of view.

Perkins, Pheme. 1984. *The Johannine Epistles*. Rev. ed. New Testament Message 21. Wilmington, DE: Michael Glazier. — Brief commentary for nonspecialists, based on careful scholarship. Considers sin and atonement rather than Christology the central issue behind 1 John.

Schnackenburg, Rudolf. 1992. *The Johannine Epistles: Introduction and Commentary*. Translated by Reginald Fuller and Ilse Fuller. New York: Crossroad. — Translated from the seventh edition of a highly respected German commentary. Thorough exegetical and theological discussion, with numerous excursuses.

Schunack, Gerd. 1982. *Die Briefe des Johannes*. Zürcher Bibelkommentare, NT 17. Zurich: Theologischer Verlag. — Relatively compact treatment providing helpful exegetical discussions.

Smalley, Stephen S. 1984. *1, 2, 3 John*. WBC 51. Waco, TX: Word. — Comprehensive, detailed, and balanced, with thorough coverage of previous scholarship. Holds that 1 John combats two different groups of opponents.

Smith, D. Moody. 1991. *First, Second, and Third John*. Interpretation. Louisville: John Knox. — Brief but helpful and exegetically reliable guide for students, teachers, and clergy, relating the meaning of the text to faith and life.

Stott, John R. W. 1988. *The Letters of John: An Introduction and Commentary*. 2d ed. Tyndale New Testament Commentaries. Grand Rapids, MI: Eerdmans. — Meant for the general reader, but with thorough and careful discussions from an evangelical point of view.

Strecker, Georg. 1996. *The Johannine Letters: A Commentary on 1, 2, and 3 John*. Translated by Linda M. Maloney. Edited by Harold Attridge. Hermeneia. Minneapolis: Fortress. — Translation of a 1989 German commentary, very thorough in its exegesis. Presents a questionable hypothesis that 2 and 3 John defend chiliasm, 1 John came later, and the Gospel of John was written last.

Thompson, Marianne Meye. 1992. *1–3 John*. IVP New Testament Commentary. Downers Grove, IL: InterVarsity. — Solid and accessible exegesis from an evangelical point of view, grounded in critical scholarship. Intended for students, pastors, and Bible teachers.

Vouga, François. 1990. *Die Johannesbriefe*. HNT 15/III. Tübingen: Mohr-Siebeck. — Very concise and compressed, but with excellent references to other ancient texts. Regards the epistles as written from a Gnostic standpoint against the developing orthodox church.

Wengst, Klaus. 1978. *Der erste, zweite und dritte Brief des Johannes*. Ökumenischer Taschenbuchkommentar zum Neuen Testament 16. Gütersloh: Gütersloher Verlagshaus Gerd Mohn; Würzburg: Echter Verlag. — Relatively brief, but quite thorough in exegesis. One of the best German commentaries, forceful and penetrating in its theological and ethical insights.

Westcott, Brooke Foss. 1892. *The Epistles of St John: The Greek Text with Notes and Essays*. 3d ed. Cambridge, England: Macmillan. — A classic and learned work of British scholarship, whose careful and lucid discussions are still worth consulting.

# INDEX

abiding, 39, 62-63, 81-84, 88, 91, 105, 107, 108, 119-20, 123-24, 155
antichrist. *See also* eschatology, opponents, 77-78, 83, 90, 110, 111, 154
atonement, 55-56, 118
authority, 28, 43, 84, 148, 158, 162

baptism, 23, 56, 79, 86, 132
"the beginning,"
    meaning of, 46-47, 64, 72, 97, 98

Cerinthus, 23-24, 80
children
    of the devil, 41, 87, 90, 93-95, 97-98
    of God, 37, 41-42, 86-87, 89-91, 93-96, 98, 127-28, 141-42
    little, 53, 70-71, 83, 160
Christology. *See also* docetism, incarnation, Jesus Christ, opponents, 22-25, 34-37, 39, 48, 69, 80-81, 106-7, 111-12, 114-15, 121, 127, 129, 135-36, 143, 146, 149, 152-54, 156
church, 28-29, 42-43, 83, 148, 158-60, 164
commandments, 60-62, 64, 105-6, 108-9, 127-29, 149-52
confession
    of Jesus Christ, 23, 81, 106, 111-12, 119-20, 153
    of sins, 54
covenant, new, 61-62, 73, 83, 92, 119

darkness. *See* light (contrasted with darkness)
Dead Sea Scrolls. *See* Qumran
death, 99, 102, 139-40, 145
Demetrius, 27, 158, 163
determinism, 41, 95
devil, 72-73, 76, 90, 93, 95, 97-98, 110-11, 114, 129, 142-43, 146
Diotrephes, 26-29, 158-59, 162

discernment formula, 31, 60-61, 100, 103, 107, 116, 128
docetism. *See also* opponents, 22-24, 80, 100, 112
dualism, 25, 40-41, 51, 73, 76, 141-43, 145

elder, 19, 26-29, 33-34, 148, 158-59, 162
eschatology. *See also* antichrist, life (eternal), parousia, 38, 42, 64-65, 68, 75, 77-78, 88-89, 94, 122, 153-54
ethics. *See also* love, sin, 34-35, 38-39, 57-58, 69, 94, 100, 102
evil one. *See* devil

faith, 35, 38, 69, 102, 107-9, 130
falsehood. *See* lie, truth (separation of from falsehood)
fellowship, 48-49, 52-53
flesh, 22-23, 25, 36, 74, 111-12, 115, 153

Gaius, 27, 29, 158-59, 161
Gnosticism. *See also* opponents, 23-24, 40, 91, 93, 143
God
    claims of seeing, 89, 162
    knowing personally, 36, 61, 67, 72-73, 76, 123-24
    love of, 62, 73, 119
    nature of, 39, 50-51, 104, 117, 123
    relation of to Christians, 36-67, 81, 105, 116, 143

hatred. *See* love (and hatred)
heresy. *See* opponents
"hinge" elements, 33, 102-3, 128, 138
honor, 28-29
hospitality, 26-29, 155-56, 159-63

Ignatius, 22, 100

# INDEX

imitation of God or of Jesus, 38, 52-53, 60, 63, 68-69, 86-87, 90, 95, 100, 105, 118, 122

incarnation. *See also* Christology, Jesus Christ, 36-37, 47, 87, 111-12, 114-15, 130, 137, 146, 153

Jesus Christ. *See also* Christology, incarnation, 36-37, 91
blood of, 55, 132-33
death of, 18, 25, 36, 55, 123, 132-33, 137
divinity of, 22, 25, 36, 112, 115, 121
humanity of, 22, 25, 36-37, 107, 112, 114-15, 121-23
as mediator, 18, 40, 105, 119
name of, 106, 161
Johannine community, 18, 21, 24, 28, 42-43, 52, 78-79, 106
John, Gospel of, 18, 20-21, 23-24, 38-40, 42, 46, 50-51, 56, 63, 89, 94, 98, 105, 118-19, 132, 135, 150
joy, 48, 155-56
judgment, day of. *See also* eschatology, 42, 122

letters, early Christian, 34, 147-48, 157, 160-61, 163-64
grammatical difficulties, 18, 45-46, 64-65, 80, 82, 87-88, 103-4, 111-12, 125, 134, 150-51, 153
life, eternal. *See also* eschatology, 42, 47, 49, 81-82, 99, 135-37, 143-44
light
contrasted with darkness, 50-54, 57-58, 64-66
love, 25, 35, 37-39, 41, 49, 51, 65, 68-69, 86-87, 94-96, 99-102, 108-9, 116-20, 123-24, 127-30, 152, 156, 159, 164
as commandment of God, 39, 60, 62, 105
of God, 62, 73, 119
and hatred, 66-67, 97, 99, 126
of one another, 37-38, 66-68, 102, 106, 117, 150
lying. *See also* truth and falsehood, 52, 78, 80-81

mission, 27, 38, 114-15, 144, 146, 155, 161, 164

non-Johannine Christianity, 21, 40, 54-56, 78, 82, 88-89, 99, 127, 130, 154, 160-61, 163

opponents. *See also* antichrist, docetism, Gnosticism, 21-25, 48, 53, 55, 75, 78-81, 89, 91, 93-94, 98-99, 106-7, 109, 111-15, 128, 132-33, 140, 143-145, 154

Papias, 19
parenesis, 31, 34, 63, 71, 97, 147, 162-63
parousia. *See also* eschatology, 18, 87-88
Polycarp, 30
prayer, 39, 105, 107-8, 139-40
purpose
of 1 John, 25, 32-33, 54, 138, 141
of 2 John, 26, 33, 148, 153-54, 156
of 3 John, 27, 28-29, 158-59

Qumran, 40, 66, 114, 143

revelation, 35-36, 39, 47, 65, 69, 87, 118-20, 123, 132-33, 143, 146, 162
rhetorical strategy, 31, 53, 56, 60-61, 79, 81, 83, 99, 113, 125, 139, 148
righteousness
of God or Jesus, 55, 86-87
human, 86-87, 95-96

Satan. *See* devil
sectarianism, 37-38, 40, 43, 89, 145
sin. *See also* ethics, 41, 53-54, 58, 67, 86, 90-94, 96, 139-42, 145
forgiveness of, 55, 72, 139
Spirit
Holy, 24-25, 43-44, 56, 79, 84, 107, 109-10, 114, 119, 120, 136
of truth, 44, 79, 114, 132-33

teachers, 83, 110
testimony, 44, 47-49, 120, 132-36, 160, 163
tradition, 23-24, 43-44, 47-49, 84, 89, 91, 98, 114, 127, 133, 136-37, 150, 156
travel. *See* hospitality, mission
truth, 58, 65, 103, 148-49, 159-61
separation of from falsehood, 52, 80, 143-45

walking, 51, 67, 148, 151
wealth, 74-75, 100-102
world, 40-41, 57, 73-76, 89, 113, 118, 129, 142-43, 145-46